PRAISE
THE TRUTH IN

Powerful and captivating! In this well-written memoir, Oriana Allen articulately conveys her story leading up to and walking through the process of being diagnosed with borderline personality disorder. She invites readers to take an intimate peak behind the curtain at her journey through heartbreak onto the path of healing, offering them hope and courage to face their own trauma-related demons. Her experience is a testimony, from someone who has walked in those shoes, to the fact that a diagnosis of BPD does not have to be a life sentence. This is an inspiring read for anyone whose life has been touched in some way by the diagnosis.

—Dr. Jeff Riddenbach PhD., Author of
Borderline Personality Disorder Toolbox: A practical Evidence-based Guide to Regulating Intense Emotions

Oriana Allen shares the painful story of her childhood with incredible warmth and candor. Then, she walks us through the process of facing that pain, owning her diagnoses of borderline personality disorder, and beginning her healing journey. Through it all, you will learn about attachment, avoidance, emptiness, and trauma firsthand through the voice of a person who has experienced it all. Whether you have a borderline diagnosis yourself, would like to better understand a loved one, or just want to learn about this complex problem, once you have read this book, you will never view borderline personality in quite the same way again.

—Jonice Webb, Ph.D., Bestselling Author of *Running on Empty: Overcome Your Childhood Emotional Neglect* and *Running on Empty No More: Transform Your Relationships.*

.

THE TRUTH IN OUR SCARS

THE TRUTH IN OUR SCARS

UNTANGLING TRAUMA TO DISCOVER YOUR SECRET SELF

ORIANA ALLEN

Published by Author Academy Elite
PO Box 43, Powell, OH 43065

www.AuthorAcademyElite.com

Identifiers:
LCCN: 2021901247
ISBN: 978-1-64746-696-1 (paperback)
ISBN: 978-1-64746-697-8 (hardback)
ISBN: 978-1-64746-698-5 (ebook)

Available in paperback, hardback, e-book

All Scripture quotations, unless otherwise indicated, are taken from the *New World Translation of the Holy Scriptures*®, Published by the Watchtower Bible Tract Society© Pennsylvania, 2013 Edition. The content of this book is in no way sponsored or endorsed by the Watch Tower and Bible Tract Society.

Any Internet addresses (websites, blogs, etc.) and telephone numbers printed in this book are offered as a resource. They are not intended in any way to be or imply an endorsement by Author Academy Elite, nor does Author Academy Elite vouch for the content of these sites and numbers for the life of this book.

Some names and identifying details have been changed to protect the privacy of individuals.

AUTHOR'S NOTE

This book is a non-fiction story, recalling very personal details of my life to the best of my memory. For the protection of people's identities, some names have been changed. Please know that I feel no malice toward anyone in this book. The stories I chose to share were carefully selected to aid the reader in understanding complex trauma and my development of borderline personality disorder. This book is also meant to guide the reader through the rigorous journey of various therapy modalities and spiritualty that supported my recovery. My ultimate goal is to share hope that recovery from borderline personality disorder is possible and to give evidence that everyone has the power within to heal and change their life's story.

ACKNOWLEDGMENTS

With the help of many people, I was able to breathe life into this book and share this raw story of transformation with you. Here is where I'd like to express a few words of gratitude for those who nurtured this journey.

From the very beginning, my husband Tom cheered me on and gave me space and time (and a shoulder to cry on at the best of times) to support the labored writing process. Having had no previous formal writing experience, I am thankful to Norma Hoyle, who helped me through a mentorship and editing my book chapter by chapter, throughout the first few years of the books growing pains.

My Kickstarter campaign was the next step that enabled me to offer pre-sales of my book to those who believed in its purpose and wanted to see it come to fruition. I am indebted to the very talented photographer, Moriah Cummings, who took a chance on me and created my book trailer for this Kickstarter project. There are many people who participated in the campaign through purchasing early copies, and I am so grateful for all of you. I am sending a special thank you to both Blake Coss and Tracy Drott for your generous campaign pledges and unswerving faith in my book. The funds raised through pre-sales enabled me to join an incredible team at Author Academy Elite and receive further coaching and opportunities in my writing career. This is where I met the very talented team of editors who I'd like to thank for their invaluable input and editorial skills, Tina Morlock and Sandra Duclos.

Last but not least, I'd like to express my deep gratitude to the skilled psychiatrist who had been like a guiding compass throughout my recovery, leading me back home to my authentic self.

DEDICATION

I dedicate this book to my loving husband
who showed me vulnerability can be a superpower
and my children, who are my life-saving miracles.
To all who have been a part of my journey in one form or
another.
For those overcoming trauma and in search of their truth.
And to my beloved and never forgotten:

Brother: Joel Meehan
1979–2012

Dad: Russell Rogers
1940–2019

Friend: Kaila McKay
1987–2020

TABLE OF CONTENTS

PART 2: LETTING THE SCARS SPEAK

PART 3: LIVING YOUR TRUTH

INTRODUCTION

DIGGING FOR BURIED TREASURE

Childhood . . . that is when we should make some of our best memories. It is when we have the freedom to live in the moment worry-free—to play, imagine, discover, build, and create. During childhood, we can be innocent and vulnerable, and we can have trust, feel secure, and fully depend on the adults in our lives. The opposite was true for me. Childhood was a time I felt robbed of and have resented. Reflecting on my childhood and adolescence reminds me of some of the worst years of my life. I buried those childhood memories deep for many years until my life depended on uncovering them. Digging through the emotional pit of trauma—like digging a hole in the earth—took much time and exertion, getting my hands dirty, and straining to see what was at the bottom. After much digging, I found a treasure—*my truth.*

This mental digging work began in adulthood after a failed suicide attempt when they hospitalized and diagnosed me with borderline personality disorder (BPD). This diagnosis forced me out of my habit of burying things and had me unearthing them instead. BPD was a label that sparked my curiosity, and I had a keen interest in learning how I developed such a disorder. To accomplish this quest, I had to revisit the place I tried to forget: my past.

With the help of a skilled psychiatrist, I was equipped with the right tools to dig through my past. I spent the first few years of recovery learning how my early interactions with my parents left a lasting imprint that set me up for a difficult future. For most of my past, I lived without ever feeling fully alive.

Childhood abuse and neglect had given me a role in the script of life that defined who I *thought* I was. This digging work in my therapy comprised of uprooting false beliefs and discovering gems of truth that revealed my secret-self. By sharing some of the work we did, you will learn how I developed a dysfunctional personality and join me on my healing journey.

In this book, I share my personal story to help you find yours.

PART 1

UNTANGLING THE PAST

1

HOME—THE BATTLEFIELD

The way our parents treated us as children
in large part determines how we treat ourselves as adults.

—Jonice Webb, *Running on Empty*

One of my earliest memories is when I was around age four. I was standing on the edge of my bed, and my eyes were level with Mom, who was standing on the floor facing me. "Close your eyes," I said to her. I puckered my lips to kiss her cheek gently. Suddenly, my inner voice interrupted my follow-through: *Don't kiss her—think of all the horrible things she's done to you.*

Slap! My hand reflexively hit my mother's face. Confusion about how it had happened overwhelmed me, but I had no time to rectify my action. Mom threw me down on the bed and held me on my side while laying multiple slaps on my thigh. Although I couldn't recall much of the physical abuse before age four, a part of me must have remembered—the part of me who couldn't bring myself to kiss my mother as I had intended. It was late at night. Struck with intense feelings of sorrow and helplessness, I jumped out of my bedroom window from our ground-level apartment. With the darkness all around me, I headed for the dimly lit playground where I had found an abandoned shopping cart. I crawled inside and looked up at the stars. I saw bright beams of light streaking back and forth across the sky. Thinking they were angels, I broke into tears and wailed, "Why? Why? Why?" I spent nearly all night in that metal cart, my knees pressed into my chest in a fetal position, pleading with those angels for answers and weeping over feelings I could neither describe nor understand.

Within the year, I turned five and moved to a new apartment complex. I packed and carried my feelings of despair with me. My nighttime escapes continued. One night, fleeing my home in the dark, the rain drenched me from head to toe. Swerving through the maze of the surrounding buildings and pathways. I was blinded by car headlights in a facing parking lot. Someone exited the vehicle and approached me, offering to help. I felt delighted the kind stranger came to my aid, but I felt simultaneously angry because I knew they had to return me to my home.

I tried to spend most of my time outdoors. My two older brothers—seven and nine years older than I—had their own interests, so I played a lot with my cousin, Greg, who was the same age as me and lived nearby. We spent a lot of time together climbing trees, in-line skating, making forts, and roaming through the many other surrounding building complexes. On an ordinary day, a man I didn't know invited me into his apartment. He led me to a bedroom. There was no furniture in the room, only magazines and pictures spread all over the floor. Standing in the middle of the room, I noticed all the people in the photos were naked. I got a sick feeling in my stomach. I knew exactly what those images were and what the people in them were doing.

Like so many of my childhood memories, the events of that day are fragmented, and I can't remember anything beyond that point. What I remember is that sick feeling in my belly—the same feeling I got when the sounds and similar images of my parents having sex in my room awakened me. Mom shared a bedroom with me. She had explained to me, "Every man is a predator and a pedophile," and she had to protect me from my father who, she believed, would come and have sex with me in the night. Mom often told me stories from her childhood, relaying graphic portrayals of men who had sexually assaulted her. She explicitly mentioned "Mike," a twenty-two-year-old married man with two kids. He had taken her—when she was twelve—to a hotel room and raped her. I didn't know Mike, but later, he became a part of my life.

I was halfway through third grade when we moved again, where I started a new school and roamed a new neighborhood. When Mom was unable to care for me, as was often the case, my brother, Jason, took over the responsibility. My eldest brother, Joel, had been suffering at the hands of an opioid addiction and engaged frequently in crimes to afford his habit. This kept him going through a revolving door of institutions. Since they were teenagers, my brothers spent as much time away from home as they could. The Ministry of Child Protective Services apprehended my cousin, Greg, from his mother's home and placed him in our care to live with us. My aged and ill grandmother was also living with us. Dad worked a lot, so Mom often took primary care of us. Days with her comprised endless chores and caretaking of her and Nana's needs. Mom yelled and hit, causing my chronic feelings of dread and terror. With each heavy thump of Mom's foot as she approached, I cowered in place, anticipating the beating to come. I longed for Dad's return home from work each day to rescue me, knowing Mom wouldn't dare hit me in front of him.

My parents consumed a lot of alcohol, which frequently led them to fight. I became familiar with and came to dread the look on Mom's face: a blank look in her eyes and bright rosy cheeks. The tone in which she groaned my name made me cringe with fear, and the loudness at night often kept me awake. I came out of my room, rubbing my eyes, only to have my mother quickly dart at me in a rage, slapping my thighs and shoving me back into my room. In the morning, I was often on my own. Dad had already gone to work, and Mom was asleep in her stupor. I had to walk a long distance to school, and I arrived late on most days. It wasn't long before the principal removed me from my class. I dreaded every step I took while walking down the broad staircase toward his office.

The principal looked frustrated and said, "Out of every person in the entire school, you have been late the most—you are late almost every day!" I was in trouble again. Classroom time was mostly a blur. I recall feeling spaced-out, making a concentrated effort to listen to the teacher's instructions, only to awaken from a daydream, frustrated and confused. I began losing myself in art projects and goofing off, eating liquid glue to get a rise out of my classmates.

One day, my class was exchanging cards and gifts on Valentine's Day. I was excited to bring home the new matching beaded necklace and bracelet I received from a boy. Mom, who was sitting at the table with that same blank look in her eyes, spotted my gift.

"Did you have to fuck him for it?"

"No!" I screamed, pulled the gift out of sight, and fled to my room. My excitement turned into shame. This boy's affection meant everything to me since I felt little of it at home.

My mother insisted I could not date until I was at least nineteen because of her fear of men. All the while, she continued to insert a wedge between my father and me. Dad had made it clear he didn't love Mom and only stayed in the picture for me. Mom's resentment poisoned her relationship with me, and she often scolded me if I said or did anything that reminded her of Dad. "Stop doing that! Your father does that!" Still, it came as a shock to me when Dad no longer lived at home with us, and we had minimal contact.

One evening, my brother, Joel, had returned home momentarily. He and Mom were arguing over something. I recall Mom hurling angry words at me.

"You little bitch," she said. Then, I felt the sting of a slap across my face.

"Don't you ever hit my little sister again!" Joel screamed. He went into a fit of rage and began kicking and smashing her belongings. He head-butted the wall with such force that he knocked himself unconscious for a few minutes. My body trembled violently, and with my fists clenched, I screamed.

"Stop it, you stupid!" My high-pitched, squealing voice cracked as I uttered the words.

Those types of fights seemed to happen less often when Greg and I saw less of Mom. For weeks at a time, she left us at home with my disabled, bed-ridden Nana to fend for ourselves. When Mom returned, she explained she was at an old friend's place. His name was Mike. This piqued my curiosity.

"Is that the same man you told me raped you when you were young?" I asked.

"No, he didn't rape me. I was just too young to understand."

Feeling confused and too afraid to question her further, I eventually met Mike when he arrived at our home with heavy chains. Mom and Mike used the chains to lock up the deep freezer and kitchen cupboards so Greg and I didn't have access to the contents inside. Mom had accused Greg of stealing and selling our food to his mother, with whom my dad was living as roommates. Days passed, and I was hungry and alone. Sometimes my brother, Jason, returned home, walked to Mike's house to get the key to the padlocks, returned to unlock the cupboards and get food for us, and then he had

7

to walk the key back to Mom. Joel came home randomly, and when he saw the chains, he lost his cool. Cursing and yelling, he tried to find something to break the locks off the chains, but he was unsuccessful.

One evening, Mike and Mom came home heavily intoxicated. Mike entered my nana's room, bent on one knee, and spoke to her in her bed. I overheard their muffled conversation. Addressing Nana, Mike said, "You're the reason she's so fucked up." He was referring to my mother. His statement triggered Mom into a fit of rage, and I was in the crossfire. Picking up a large kitchen knife and holding it over my head, Mom yelled, "I'm going to kill you, you little bitch" while she lunged at me. Filled with terror, I bolted around her and through the hallway where she chased me. My heart was beating so fast I thought it would come right out of my chest. Those seconds felt like an eternity. The rest of the incident was a blur, and I recalled only the moments after the incident. I was sitting on the back porch watching them leave in Mikes truck, knees to my chest, profusely crying, while Greg was nervously laughing at me.

Life drastically changed thereafter. By age eleven, they removed Greg from our home—he went into foster care in another city—and they sent Nana up North a few hours away to live at my aunt's place. Mom had broken the news to me: we were moving into Mikes place. Having little help or money, we moved most of our belongings with a shopping cart. We loaded our possessions into the cart, walked several blocks to unload, and repeated the trip several times. Contact with my dad ceased altogether since Mike was around. On my birthday, Dad had picked me up from school and walked me part of the way home. He gave me a card that I proudly showed Mom. This angered her and led her to further target my father's relationship with me. Mom told my schoolteacher and principal that my dad was a sex offender and demanded they not allow him on school property. Our visits ended and the phone calls were few, but Mom promised I could see Dad on the upcoming Christmas Day.

In the meantime, Mike and I were not getting along. When he spoke to me, he often mocked my responses and called me stupid. He then talked to me using a distorted sounding voice and mimicked sign language, implying I wouldn't understand what he was saying. Because of the frequent humiliation, I feared ridicule and developed selective mutism, a severe anxiety disorder where I could not speak in certain circumstances. He then referred to me as the "deaf-dumb mute." In my loneliness, I was happy when I received a phone call from Greg.

"Do you like Mike?" he asked.

"Yeah," I said. But my response was reflexive, and I quickly corrected myself in a whisper in case anyone heard.

"No!"

We both shared a giggle. Immediately after, the sound of thumping feet approached my bedroom, and the door swung open. Mom knocked me down on the bed and hit me repeatedly, and I quickly realized she had been listening on the line.

Smash! The sound of shattering glass awakened me in the early morning hours. It scared me too much to come out of my bedroom or to peek out at what had happened. The police arrived shortly, and I learned my dad had arrived at the house, kicked in the sliding glass door, and demanded to see me. I had heard rumors Dad stole a photograph of me from the wall before Mike had kicked him down the winding stairs, where the police charged him with mischief. Not long after this incident, Christmas came, and I eagerly waited to call my dad. I started my morning at the tree with the few presents I had received, all wrapped in dish cloths and old newspapers and tied together with rope. With Mike staring at me as I opened my gifts, I forced a smile. My best friend from school, Jewel, phoned:

"So, what did you get?" she asked.

I tried to sound enthusiastic about my presents, hiding my disappointment of the day. She went on to tell me about all the nice things she'd received. The day wore on, but Mom denied me the opportunity to call or visit my dad. I spent the next few nights at Jewel's, and while we lay in her waterbed, her Aunt Trina came and sat at my beside. Placing her hand on my head and caressing my hair, she spoke gently when she told me Dad had attempted suicide on Christmas Day by swallowing several pills. She said they saved him, and she assured me he would be okay and was recovering in the hospital.

Back home, my mother seemed to worship the ground Mike walked on. I felt unseen. The more she fought for his affection, the more unloved I felt. Watching her favor him over me, even after witnessing how he mistreated me, I felt betrayed. He was always right in her opinion, resulting in her prompt compliance with his demands, and it produced an empty feeling that gnawed at me. While spending the next few days at Jewel's, I sat on the floor of her bedroom, looking into her vanity mirror. I stared at my face with disgust. *You're so ugly—nobody likes you.* It was the first time I fantasized about how I would take my life.

Jewel had become everything to me, the center of my world, and I clung to her like a shadow. I confided much of my home life to her, often meeting her at school and showing her the welts my mom left on my legs. Her aunt started a journal, one where I logged each time my mother put her hands on me. Many of the nights I spent there, Jewel and I visited the man downstairs—a family friend living in their basement suite. He let us sleep in his bed, often lying beside us in his underwear. Some nights, he awakened me by rubbing his erection against my body and fondling me. I lay awake while pretending to be asleep and slowly tried to move my arm toward Jewel to nudge her awake, hoping it would make him stop. As this continued to happen undetected, I believed what my mother said about men was true. Jewel and I talked about the molestation. We became convinced we would never want to be with a man and would move out and live together forever. Then, we became intimately involved with each other. In time, my relationship with Jewel reflected the dynamic I had with my mother. With no boundaries, Jewel became overly controlling and envious, and I endured her verbal and physical attacks.

By age twelve, I began showing signs of aggression, damaging property, binge drinking alcohol, and smoking cigarettes. Another neighborhood friend let me sleep over sometimes. During these stays, we sneaked into her parents' room, stole the car keys from her mother's purse, and took her car on a joy ride, sometimes all night. I used substances and rebellious thrills to escape my tormented feelings of rejection. Jewel's Aunt continued to look after me. Knowing where I had come from, she often made excuses for my disruptive behavior, saying, "You know she is a problem child." I wore the label well, as I had always felt I was exactly that—someone's problem.

Adolescence—The War of Chaos and Perfectionism

Upon entering High school, I was old enough to choose where I wanted to live. I was ecstatic to move out of Mom and Mike's place and into an apartment with Dad. For a while, things felt good at home. Dad purchased a new stereo for me and gave me the freedom to have friends over. For my fourteenth birthday, at my request, he purchased the alcohol for my friends and me when I hosted my first house party.

I asked Dad to leave the apartment, and because he wanted to please me, he left us to do as we wished. The night carried on recklessly, resulting in many vomiting teenagers and damaged belongings. Nights like these continued because Dad had been more of a friend than a guiding parent. My binge-drinking to the point of blacking out was an escape I had engaged in often. This so-called escape had become more like my prison as it continued to take control over my life. As my destructive behaviors increased, my relationship with Jewel ended, and I surrounded myself with people who were as lost and destructive as I was.

On one of these heavily intoxicated nights at a new acquaintance's place, I drank until I lost consciousness. In the night, I awoke to the sound of a young man's voice saying, "I'm finished!" As I came to my senses, my confusion lifted as I felt the pelvic pains of what he had done, and I cried, knowing he had violated me. He had taken the only innocence I had left, leaving another piece of my soul stolen. Attending my tenth-grade class on autopilot the following morning, I felt disconnected from myself and others and knew I was never going to be the same; I lost the will to care about myself at all. Shortly afterward, I dropped out of school and began dating a boy who had been into drugs, crime, and in prison several times. After one of our phone conversations had ended in an argument, I couldn't bear the feelings of rejection. I locked myself in the bathroom and used my shaving razor to cut myself, leaving bloodstains in the sink and bathtub. Dad saw the mess and called an ambulance, and they took me to the hospital. As they bandaged my arm, rage washed over me because I realized the pain of my existence was still with me. I fled the hospital in my bare feet, ripping off the bandages as I ran toward home.

Back at home, Dad's hero status faded as his flaws revealed themselves. His personal demon of alcoholism accompanied his permissive parenting style. Often, I came home from school only to be locked out. Waiting for several hours, I had nothing to do but think about how little I mattered. *Dad's at the bar again . . . he forgot about me again.* On other occasions, Dad's buddies from the local dingy bar were over regularly, drinking in our cigarette-smoke-filled home. Those evenings usually ended in arguments, with me being forced to leave the house—often in the middle of the night. Sometimes, I slept in the park or in an unused storage locker of an apartment building.

On one of these evenings of Dad's drinking bouts, I heard a woman shriek in a slurred voice, "Where's my money?" I cracked open my bedroom door and saw a woman dressed in black lingerie, swaying back and forth with her hands inside her underwear, groping herself. Repulsed with what I had seen, I stayed in my room, trying to block out the sounds of the services she was performing for Dad and his friend. But when I heard the woman crying, I could not ignore it. I left my bedroom and found the woman sitting on our kitchen floor with a knife in her hand. Realizing she had cut her wrists multiple times, I got down on my knees and held her arm still while I removed the knife from her hand. When I asked her what was wrong, she wailed fiercely and said her son had recently committed suicide, and she didn't want to live anymore. I sat with her on the kitchen floor as she poured out her heart, and I listened with deep empathy and compassion because I knew what it felt like to want to die.

My brother, Joel, had come back into the picture, still in the grips of his addiction, and almost daily, he and his friends brought home stolen goods to sell for their drug use. Between Dad, Joel, and the steady traffic of drug-addicted people in and out of our home, they stole many of our belongings and sold them: the new stereo Dad bought me upon moving in, my movies, games, jewelry, and clothing. Begging Joel to stop,

I threatened him with suicide if he didn't quit using drugs. So, my choose-me-over-your-drugs pattern of codependency began—one that had followed me into my future relationships.

After Joel's actions caught up with him, he was arrested and served time in jail. While home alone one afternoon, three men opened the door. While entering, they chuckled. "You know, you should really keep your door locked." They asked for Joel's whereabouts, wanted what he had stolen from them, and threatened me not to phone the police, or they would hold me accountable for the stolen items they wanted returned. They searched the home, flipping over mattresses and pulling the house apart. I knew they were looking for the marijuana Joel had ripped off from a grow operation, and I knew where he stashed it. I ran into the bathroom and noticed they had cut our home phone lines and threw them in the toilet bowl.

One man yelled, "Get in the closet!" as he shoved me into it. The closet had been crammed full of stuff, and I couldn't fit, so I pleaded to sit on the couch. I watched them ransack the house until they found the marijuana. They left with what they came for, and I was relatively unharmed.

Drugs, violence, crime and perverted sex were the staples of my life, along with chronic feelings of abandonment, betrayal, invalidation, and loneliness. With a general feeling of unease and unpredictability, desperately trying to relieve my despair, I asked a local drug user who frequented our home to let me try his drugs. He tossed me a small folded paper that held a portion of white powder inside and invited me to his home, which a friend and I later visited. Sitting around his kitchen table, he passed us a glass pipe with a crystal-like substance inside. After he showed us how to smoke it, time seemed to fast-forward, and the night quickly turned into day. As days like this came and went, the man then cut us off from his free, steady supply of drugs, leaving us utterly hooked and in the grips of withdrawal. The battle with this addiction had begun.

Approaching age seventeen, I was unrecognizable. The person I had become was shocking to people who knew me previously. After many encounters with the police, such as car accidents resulting from high-speed police chases in stolen vehicles and recurring physical fights with others, I was arrested and placed on probation. I attended counseling through court order, which started my self-awakening: the realization that I had to (and wanted to) change for the better. To escape the chaos that surrounded me, I returned to the last place I ever thought I would . . . my mother's. Mom had separated from Mike and was actively participating in a Bible study program. I packed a suitcase and crashed on Mom's couch, where I detoxed for the next week. Mostly drifting in and out of sleep, a piercing ache in my bones awakened me, and I was shivering from a coldness that felt as if I were in a wicked snowstorm. When I awakened in a pool of cold sweat, Mom placed the food she had prepared in front of me, and I shoveled it down as if I hadn't seen food in years, only to fall asleep in exhaustion again. After the physical detoxing was complete, I awoke and felt surprisingly well, like a heavy cloud had lifted. Although I noticed a significant, positive change in Mom, I knew I couldn't stay there, and going back to my dad's place was no longer an option.

Facing homelessness, I applied for and received some government financial assistance earmarked for youth. It provided me only enough money to pay rent—nothing else. I used this support to move into a small basement suite of my own. Living off this government assistance and food stamps, I tried to go back to school part time and find employment. Unable to secure employment, my unruly behavior resulted in being shuffled around to six different high schools and having to move residences twice. I couldn't seem to gain any control over my life.

My mother called to inform me of what I believed was a life-changing opportunity. She explained to me that our family, who lived in the countryside a few hours farther north, had found a place to rent, suggesting we move there and live together. Mom and I agreed to go, and she would support me so I could finish high school. So, with the support from our family, we moved and settled into our new, small home in the countryside. I started high school and quickly realized how little I fit in—I couldn't relate to anyone. One evening while hanging out with some of my cousins and their friends, I retold the story of how we were so poor we had used coffee filters (received from the food bank) for toilet paper. My cousin privately approached me and discouraged me from sharing those kinds of stories. Realizing I couldn't share most things about myself or my past—and not being able to withstand the rejection of my new peers—I adapted. I completely suppressed the person I was (the one who came from chaos), which resulted in me becoming the extreme opposite of myself—a perfectionist. The war within between chaos and perfectionism was born.

My new high-achiever-self earned the acceptance of my teachers and peers, which reinforced her existence. This helped me maintain an approved place in society. It was as if my former life, with all its pain and chaos, had never existed; I put it all behind me. In this new environment, where no one really knew me or where I came from (only the current self I portrayed), I thought I had it all together—and in that life, I was perfect.

I was an honor roll student approaching graduation, reg-istered for a college course as an aesthetician after graduation, and knew my parents had an education fund set aside for me. When I asked my mother about the fund, she explained Dad hadn't contributed financial support since their separation; therefore, the money rightly belonged to her. I did not agree, of course, but I needed to pay for my fast-approaching classes. So, we went to the bank to settle matters. Given my naïveté and Mom's cunning, she convinced me to sign the education fund over to her name. I never received the funds and soon after applied for a student loan.

Upon learning Mike and my mother had reunited, I also discovered she gave the funds to him to help him with legal matters regarding his family property. When I confronted her about the unfairness of what she had done, Mom justified her actions by saying Mike had used a portion of the money to buy me a graduation dress and had paid for some of my dance lessons. She viewed that as a noble act of kindness on his part. Despite how far I had come from my past, I was reminded, yet again, how Mike came before me in Mom's heart.

2

THE COLLAPSE—DIAGNOSED

I'm so good at beginnings, but in the end
I always seem to destroy everything, including myself.

—Kiera Van Gelder, *The Buddha and the Borderline*

After my mother had moved back to our former city, I stayed behind to create a new life, working in my new career and leaving the past behind, or so I thought. I spent the next few years working as an aesthetician—a job that entails pampering others. One time while working in a luxurious spa, someone referred to my role as being that of a professional relaxer—for others. In my life, however, relaxation eluded me. One day at work, a new client was enthusiastically telling me about a book she had been reading and exclaimed how interesting it was, and she said I must read it too. Upon her departure, she lent me her copy. I forgot about the book and never saw her again because I stopped working there a short while later. My life carried on, and in my busyness of juggling two (and sometimes three) jobs, I didn't take time to read the book—not until a few years later when it became very significant in my life.

I had become addicted to the busyness of life—the demands of a never-ending and self-created to-do list and the physical activity of fitness and exercise. When I wasn't working at my job or working out at the gym, I was busy in the nightlife scene, surrounding myself with people in the local bars and at house parties. Bouncing from relationship to relationship, flattery from the opposite sex temporarily seemed to soothe my chronic feeling of emptiness within. Most of my relationships were with narcissistic men, and I couldn't seem to measure up to their expectations of me. The more I tried to be what they wanted, the more the void within me grew bigger and heavier. I landed myself in somewhat of a stable relationship for a time with a man I cared intensely for, but my perfect-life façade was crumbling. The image of perfection I portrayed was nothing more than a figurative house, built for protection from the elements of my inner suffering. It housed a negative self-image constructed on a faulty foundation. And like a house built on sand, it collapsed. Although my feelings for my partner were genuine, I couldn't seem to control my destructive tendencies that damaged our relationship, which included episodes of extreme rage and black outs, often with amnesia following them.

Upon waking one morning after a night out with girl-friends, I was unable to recall my night, and I felt a sense of relief. *Oh, thank goodness nothing bad happened last night.* My partner entered the room and yelled, "Do you even remember last night? Look at your ankle; I think it's broken!" In confusion, I tried to get out of bed but fell as soon as I put pressure on my foot. Shame washed over me as he told me what he knew of my night. He said a man had knocked on our door in the middle of the night, carrying me across his arms, who explained he had found me lying in the middle of the road and thought I was a garbage bag (I was wearing a short black dress). The man expressed his relief at not running over me but said he didn't know where my pants were, and my dress had been hiked upward. Somehow, I mumbled my address to this kind man, so he drove me home. I later found my wallet and earrings in the middle of the road. A trip to the hospital established my ankle was broken, but I had no recollection of how it happened.

Nights like these continued to happen—nights that turned into days where my disappearing acts would take place for an entire weekend. During these episodes, I found all kinds of people in all the wrong places, which were filled with drinking, drugging, promiscuity, spending sprees, and dangerous driving while under the influence.

Intense shame plagued me each time I had to face the ones I hurt. My inability to explain why I did these things and why I couldn't stop, no matter how much I wanted to, exacerbated their pain. It felt like my body was being taken over by a force more powerful than I, and I had zero control. Upon learning my partner and I had become pregnant, I excitingly shared the news. Instead of the joyful reaction I anticipated, he insisted we must not follow through. With much convincing I begrudgingly complied with terminating the pregnancy. A decision that soon after haunted me. My partner eventually ended our relationship by getting involved with another woman who waitressed at a pub we frequented. The devastation of this rejection and betrayal tormented me, and at night, I often drove by his home and the pub where she worked to find his vehicle and discover his whereabouts. Unable to let go of my pain of abandonment—I persisted in drinking alcohol at a local bar to obliterate my existence, only to find his new girlfriend there. She approached me and asked me to talk to her in the bathroom. After I poured my heart out to her, confiding in her about the recent loss of our pregnancy, she took me to the bar, ordered tequila shots for us, then insisted we go together to confront my former partner at his home. When we arrived, I abruptly entered his bedroom yelling and crying. Shocked and appalled to see me, he demanded I leave. When my desperate attempt to reason with him failed, I grabbed a kitchen knife and started slashing my wrists. His frustration intensified, and he grabbed me by my hair, dragging me out of the house and into the car. We arrived at the hospital, and I received several stitches, but the pain within remained.

Soon after, I had lost my employment, my house, and my relationship. Everything I had worked so hard for I had managed to demolish. Trying to pick up the pieces of my life, I sought therapy, but after a few sessions, I had called my therapist to cancel our appointment and told her I was going to end my life. After swallowing a few bottles of over-the-counter medications, a friend had come to visit at my rented room. she could see I was not well, and after I confessed what I had done, she drove me to the hospital. My inpatient stay was a blur as my body recovered. When I was more alert, I realized I had been admitted into a psychiatric unit and wasn't allowed to leave until further examination. The attending psychiatrist evaluated me and abruptly stated, "You have borderline personality disorder! Read the book, *I Hate You, Don't Leave Me*. It was a greater shock than the diagnosis to realize this was the book my former salon client had lent me and insisted I read so many years ago! It felt surreal—I had been lugging this same book around for the last few years, unread, and never realized it was the key to a door I needed to open.

I spent the next few weeks as an inpatient, reading this book that defined everything I had been living with over the years: my fears of rejection and abandonment, my turbulent relationships and behaviors, the lack of a consistent identity, and the emptiness that gnawed inside of me. It was bizarre to read about myself in a book, feeling liberated because I had some explanations, yet ashamed I was now wearing the label of a personality disorder. During my stay at the hospital, I received a phone call on the visitor's line. Eager to learn who had called me, an unexpected voice surprised me when I answered; it was the woman my ex-partner had been dating. She informed me she was a psychiatric nurse and heard of my admission. She asked to visit me and bring me something to read. I declined her offer. After the phone call, I entered my room and lay on my bed, grief-stricken over my failed relationship and what had become of me. A nurse, who appeared to be the same age as I, had taken a liking to me. She entered my room, sat on the end of my bed, and spent much time with me, expressing how I reminded her of herself. She had kindly photocopied many self-help worksheets from a workbook and gave them to me. We had several heartfelt conversations throughout my stay, and she continued to keep me busy with self-help projects. I journaled daily about my stay there and often referred to her as "my angel" when I wrote about her.

As I had moped around the hospital, a nurse who observed my body language abruptly said, "You should be thankful that you're finding this out while still so young, instead of later on when your life is half over!" Although it was true that I had a head start on changing and recovering, I still felt lost. *What am I supposed to do now?* They gave me a label, some worksheets, and a book, then sent me on my way with no guidance on how to overcome my symptoms and challenges. While on a day pass, I went for a walk around the neighborhood with some new friends I met in the hospital. While walking past a liquor store, I gazed inside and felt a deep uneasiness. The thought of discharge began to frighten me—I feared the poor choices I'd make with my freedom, and I believed I was safer staying inside the hospital. I couldn't trust myself to control my emotions and behaviors—I was in fear of what I might do next. Believing no one had my back—not even I—made my world seem completely unsafe.

After I was released from the hospital, my mom's boyfriend, Mike, called me. Knowing of my struggles, he offered me what he thought was a generous way to help. He said he had a large bank account I could access if I came over and had a few drinks with him, and he also had $500 "wrapped up in a pink little nighty"—one I would wear for him. In my shock, confusion, and denial, I remained silent while my head was spinning, trying to wrap my head around his words but not quite grasping the message at first. After we had hung up, I realized he was propositioning me to have sex with him for money, in the guise of helping me in my dire situation. I dreaded telling my mother, thinking she would only blame and despise me more.

Feeling hopeless and tormented by thoughts that I wasn't anything more than a worthless, unlovable person, I ended up back at the bars. While socializing, I was approached by a girl. "Do you remember me?" she asked. It took a minute to register before I realized it was "my angel" from the hospital. We talked, danced, and hugged, then she grabbed my hand and pulled me into the ladies' washroom where we shared a stall. She faced the toilet seat and spread white powdered lines of cocaine across the back of the toilet to snort them and invited me to partake. Against my better judgment, my desire for acceptance won, and I complied. The night carried on at her home, well after the bar closed.

That was when she told me her best friend and coworker was the woman my ex was in a relationship with, and the familiar sting of betrayal returned, especially after I learned they had been together at her home. Flooded with angst and many questions, I couldn't help but wonder if my so-called angel had only gotten close to me to become an informant for her friend. *Is any of her friendliness toward me genuine?*

Does she care about me at all? She knows I am vulnerable; is that why she offered me drugs and invited me over? Am I being played? I still don't know the answers to these questions, but I learned from something else she had said—something that would be significant to my future recovery.

"I shouldn't be telling you this," she stated. She explained the psychiatrist who diagnosed me had held a staff meeting on my behalf when I was an inpatient at the hospital, and I had been the focus of that meeting. He asked the nurses this question about me, "Why is she different?" In response to the nurses' silence, he answered his question, stating "Because she has insight." I have never forgotten those words. And although I did not understand what that meant at the time, I wanted to understand *why* and *how* it made me different.

I've learned having insight means you can gain an accurate and deep intuitive understanding of a person or thing. In my case, the deep intuitive understanding was of my core self, and how it contributed to my illness. Insight, or what I call "in-sight"—looking in—is the key to developing self-awareness. You need insight to be introspective, to examine and observe your mental and emotional processes and make changes accordingly. It involves the ability to have a flexible perception that can see from many angles, not only from your pre-existing lens—which often gets distorted by your belief system. I can now see cause-and-effect—both on my part and by others—how they intertwine with one another and how interactions get filtered through the lens of our experiences, beliefs, and expectations. It's like working at a jig-saw puzzle, trying to fit the pieces together—a process that gives you the calming reins to your emotions with a clear and complete picture as the result.

Having this insight—and further developing it through curiosity instead of judgment—has allowed me to become a more conscious, thinking, and proactive person instead of a reactive one. Through developing such insight, you can view the world in a new way, and re-examine existing conventions that challenge the status quo.

Acquiring knowledge of my diagnosis was only the beginning. When you turn knowledge inward, you can create the personal insights needed for growth. Looking within myself for answers was much too scary, so it remained a struggle for a long time. I continued looking to others for answers, hoping to fill the void, until it became much scarier when this outlook nearly took my life.

3

TURNING POINT

If you live for people's acceptance, you'll die from their rejection.

—Lecrae Moore, *Unashamed*

The first step on this new journey was learning about borderline personality disorder, since I knew nothing about it prior to my diagnosis. To qualify for a diagnosis of borderline personality disorder, currently, you must have at least five of the nine traits listed in the American Psychiatric Association's *Diagnostic and Statistical Manual of Mental Disorders, 5ʰ Edition.1* I include these symptoms here to help you further understand the disorder, but please try to refrain from self-diagnosing yourself with any personality disorder. Only a licensed mental health professional can make that determination. Learning what traits I shared was tough to face—below is an overview:

Part 1: frantic efforts to avoid real or imagined abandonment

Part 2: a pattern of unstable and intense interpersonal relationships characterized by alternating

between extremes of idealization and
devaluation

Part 3: identity disturbance: markedly and persistently
unstable self -image or sense of self

Part 4: impulsivity in at least two areas that
are potentially self-damaging (e.g.,
spending, sex, substance abuse, reckless
driving, binge eating)

Part 5: recurrent suicidal behaviour, gestures, or
threats—or self-mutilating behaviour

Part 6: affective (emotional) instability due
to a marked reactivity of mood (e.g.,
intense episodic dysphoria, irritability,
or anxiety) usually lasting a few hours and only
rarely more than a few days

Part 7: chronic feelings of emptiness

Part 8: inappropriate, intense anger or difficulty
controlling anger (e.g., frequent displays of
temper, constant anger, or recurrent physical
fights)

Part 9: transient, stress-related paranoid ideation or
severe dissociative symptoms

These traits need to be pervasive—affecting all areas of
functionality day to day, a persistent pattern. For a long time,
reading these traits described in books were only words on
paper. Although they provided some validity for my struggles,
I couldn't make these words produce any changes in my behaviors—it was only information. Similarly, I oscillated between
group therapy, individual therapy, and regular Bible studies,
collecting information on topics such as anger management,
boundaries, relaxation and mindfulness techniques, addiction,

self-esteem, and how to reconcile myself with others and God. With all these efforts, I still lacked the ability to apply what I was learning to make lasting changes.

I moved back to my city of origin and found a place where my dad and I could live together because I needed the financial support while I pursued therapy and paid off the debts I had accrued. This arrangement worked well for a time because it enabled me to work many hours and pay my debts—Dad often complained I worked too much. This was true until I walked off the job site when my narcissistic employer—who had sexually harassed me and the other girls—swore at me in front of the other staff. I had had enough. After remaining unemployed for a while, I had given up on bettering myself and my former rebellious ways manifested again. Because I believed all was hopeless, I abandoned my aspirations of maintaining work, therapy, and spirituality. I depended on the crowd of associates who I regularly partied with for meaning and purpose in my life. This crowd gave me the permission to be my chaotic-self, which gave me an illusion of freedom. In reality, I was a slave to their acceptance. My "favorite person" (FP) belonged to this group. (FP is a term used to describe how people with BPD experience an intense attachment to a single person, one who determines my mood, identity, and self-worth.) One evening, I got into an argument with my FP over the phone. After we hung up, in my mind, the argument meant the relationship was over. I couldn't bear this thought, and I concluded if this relationship was over, I might as well die. Taking a large kitchen knife with a serrated blade, I cut my forearm and hoped it would end my life. In intense pain, I laid on the floor thinking my escape from this world and all my emotional pain wouldn't take long. As I lay there, my increasing physical pain soon turned my death wish into regret. I called my mom and screamed into the phone, "I fucked up!" repeatedly and hung up.

Thankfully, Mom knew to call an ambulance. When they arrived and entered my home, they found me in a pool of my blood on my bedroom floor. The police assisted them into my dad's room, awakened him, and took him in for questioning to rule out any foul play. Dad, who was unaware of what had happened, was escorted past my room. Upon seeing me, I could see the expression of confusion on his face turn into pure heartbreak. The ambulance brought me to the hospital emergency room where they bandaged me, and I waited for several hours to see a doctor who later stitched my wound. It wasn't until the next day that I was placed in a small interview room where I met the person who would assist me in the next few years of personal growth and witness my complete transformation.

4

THERAPY—
THE JOURNEY INWARD

*Until you make the unconscious conscious,
it will direct your life and you will call it fate.*

—C. G. Jung

D r. Vand was the psychiatrist on shift at the ER that
night. She entered the room and spoke to me, which
I can vaguely remember. Shortly after, I began weekly
individual therapy with her. Allowing myself to be vulnerable
proved to be a challenge for the first year, as I struggled to
allow myself to feel and cry in our sessions, which robbed an
entire year of progress. But like any relationship, especially
that between patient and doctor, it takes time to build trust
and develop a sense of safety and comfort, and in order to
be vulnerable, you must first feel safe. When I felt secure in
the relationship, I discovered it was through letting the scars
of my past speak, that I could explore, connect, and heal.

As I explored my vulnerabilities and gave voice to my inner
scars, I realized I spent much of my adolescence living in a

state of mental semi-consciousness. I was not fully conscious and aware of myself and my behaviors or what motivated them, it was as if I were sleep-walking through my life and operating from a deep abandonment wound. Because of child abuse and neglect over many years, I became an adult veteran suffering from a complex form of post-traumatic stress disorder (PTSD). They consider PTSD complex when chronic neglect or physical, emotional, or sexual abuse occurred during a person's developmental years, especially if the abuser was a caretaker (e.g., a parent or guardian). PTSD can cause scars in the brain's neural pathways, and it has taken many years of therapy to rewire my new neural pathways. That therapy helped me wake up from my living nightmare.

BELIEF SYSTEMS—THE STORY WE TELL OURSELVES

Life's early experiences and relationships are where we develop our inner belief system: beliefs about ourselves (self-schema), other people, the world, and our place within it. At the beginning of life, we construct schemas (mental models that serve as a framework) to create connections and make sense of our world and ourselves. As the self-schema develops, our beliefs become solidified and are fundamental to our sense of self: who we are. We see and operate from them as if they're absolute truths. Often referred to as "core beliefs," these truths shape our perceptions, interpretations, and assumptions. It is the shortcut by which we assimilate or disregard new information. We unconsciously filter this input through a confirmation bias that aligns with our core beliefs. This makes it challenging to see things differently from what we already believe them to be.

To learn what I believed about myself and my role in this world, I had to explore with curiosity to find answers to questions like these:

- Why is deciding so hard?
- Why did being honest or vulnerable seem painstaking or impossible?
- Why did I lack self-control over my emotions?
- Why did I keep making the same mistakes repeatedly?
- Why couldn't I stop destructive behaviors when I wanted to?
- Why did I obsess over others, wishing I could be as good as someone else?
- Why did I pick partners who were narcissistic, substance-dependent, and/or abusive?
- Why was I completely detached from myself, searching for my existence in others?
- Why did I believe serving others—doing as they wanted—would earn me a place in their life, improve my self-worth, and earn their love?
- Why did I believe if people knew me, they would not like me?
- Why was dying more appealing to me than living?

The answers were buried in my past. I came to understand that growing up in a home with alcoholic-addict parents left me with many of my fundamental needs unmet; therefore, I learned my needs were unimportant. Since my siblings and I could rarely be children and our parents forced us into a caretaker role to meet their needs, I learned that to earn love, I needed to care and do for others no matter the cost.

Having witnessed domestic violence and being subjected to physical, verbal, and emotional abuse, the rest of my beliefs held a negative narrative—a narrative of the story I learned to believe about myself. I call these internalized messages or stories the "lies in disguise." They sounded like this:

- I am not lovable; I need to earn love and worthiness by how much I do for people.
- I am not good enough as I am; I need to be more, do more, have more, etc.
- I must take care of others before myself.
- People always leave me, eventually; if people knew the real me, they wouldn't stay.
- It is not safe to express myself.
- My needs and wants are bad or unimportant.

My choices in life were an outward manifestation of these lies. With frustration and self-defeat, I made statements in therapy, such as "life will be always a struggle;" "I'll never be normal;" and "I'll never have a home." These thoughts and beliefs led to the feelings and actions that reflected them: chaotic, defective, and transient.

Exploration in therapy revealed many of my behaviors comprised of *constantly searching for evidence* that I was not lovable and not good enough. These fear-based beliefs led me unconsciously to choose partners who would reject and abandon me. I was drawn to other people who reinforced my beliefs and vice versa. In schema therapy, this dynamic is called a "schema chemistry." Everyone has their schema, and we choose partners who reinforce ours. Someone (like myself) who has a self-sacrificing schema (I need to give) is drawn to people who are usually narcissistic or have an entitled schema (I need to get).[2] The self-sacrificing schema that I identify with comprises of several things:

- Prioritizing taking care of others above yourself
- Feeling overly responsible for other's feelings, often putting your feelings aside
- Readily taking the blame and claiming responsibility for the behavior of others
- Struggling to ask for what you need often feeling guilty or selfish when asking
- Fearing to assert your needs to your partner; you believe they will dismiss or leave you

Subconsciously, to confirm my core beliefs, I created situations and attracted people with whom I reenacted my past. I was constantly disowning myself in favor of others because I believed it was necessary for relationships.

My doctor wisely explained that my parents, for reasons of their own, were incapable of meeting my needs, and I had to recognize the feelings of guilt are *theirs* to hold, not mine. As Dr. Vand rightly placed it: "You believe you're not good enough because you carry the scars of your parents' failure." The failures of our parents may become our burden, but it is our choice to continue carrying it onward into the next generation or put it down. My adopted beliefs were my written script for living, and I played it out like a self-fulfilling prophecy. As I moved toward healing, I learned unconscious patterns can change once brought into awareness.

5

RECYCLED RELATIONSHIPS—THE ONE THAT SHAPED ALL OTHERS

We repeat what we don't repair.

—Christine Langley-Obaugh

During my recovery journey, I discovered new truths about maternal narcissism through a book Dr. Vand recommended I read: *Will I Ever Be Good Enough? Healing the Daughters of Narcissistic Mothers* by Karyl McBride. The words I read struck me to my core because I felt as if she had written them specifically for me. The book's explanations helped me attain a true understanding of—and a healing from—the mother-daughter relationship I had fought so hard to establish. This book described my relationship with my mother and the sense of loss that consumed me almost exactly.

Reading the true stories—and responding to a questionnaire in the book—led me to discern that my relationship with my mother contained, on many levels, key elements of maternal narcissism.[3] Significant explanations that applied to me sounded like this:

- When I discuss my life issues with my mother, she diverts the discussion back to her to talk about herself.

- My mother acts jealous of my relationship with my father.

- I have questioned often if my mother even loved me.

- I felt I was a slave to my mother.

- I have felt a lack of emotional closeness with my mother.

- When I discuss my feelings, she must top them with her own.

- I believed it was my role to attend to her needs, feelings, and desires.

- The mother-daughter love I craved, I believed needed to be earned by seeing to Mom's needs and constantly doing what it took to please her.

- Mother viewed me as an extension of herself, not as an individual with my own set of feelings, desires, or identity—often resulting in boundary and privacy violations.

- Never having received validation, I felt insignificant.

- I felt valued only for what I did rather than for who I am.

- My mother acted as if the world revolved around her.

- My mother tried to control my choices.

- I had become either a high achiever or self-sabotaging.

- As a child, my mother expected me to react to her needs instead of her reacting to mine.

I had all the above statements in common with Karyl McBride's book. It defined everything I had been facing throughout my entire relationship with my Mom. Even some stories related by people in the book were identical to my own. McBride said daughters of narcissistic mothers often heard and internalized messages such as "I'm not good enough;" "I'm valued for what I do, rather than for who I am;" and "I am unlovable."[4] It was all too familiar. McBride describes the six faces of maternal narcissism. I particularly identified with "The Psychosomatic." This face worn by the mother portrays a sick woman who uses illness, aches, and pains to manipulate others, get her own way, and keep the attention on herself. This type feels entitled to be cared for, and when people do not respond to her, she uses a more intense form of playing the victim. Her approach may bring on an illness-related crisis that makes you feel guilty and redirects your attention back to her. This is what McBride describes as the "illness control method."[5]

This additional information helped me see things with clearer eyes. I no longer looked through distorted lenses or had my faulty belief system and feelings of misplaced guilt obscure my vision. I discovered this is a historic pattern, a family dynamic, which was well put by McBride when she said, "Our mothers probably hadn't gotten it (love) from their mothers, either, which means that a painful legacy of distorted love was passed from generation to generation."[6] This statement made me look at my mother's behaviors differently. It offered me further insight into understanding their origin and enabled me to view her behaviors with curiosity instead of judgment and, for the first time, with empathy. Things started to make sense, and having felt a measure of validation, I gained a different perspective on my interactions with my mother then, now, and for all other relationships in my life.

ATTACHMENT STYLES—BREAKING RELATIONSHIP PATTERNS

After learning about maternal narcissism, this was the first time I took an interest in other personality disorders aside from borderline. Through much analyzing of my relationship history and our behavior patterns, I found the narcissistic personality type described nearly all those I was in a relationship with during my adolescence. My relationships involved people who mimicked and reinforced my life's history of never proving to be good enough, my terror of the next physical attack, and the unpredictability of whether they would stay or leave. Learning beliefs and schemas play a role in choosing our partners, my next truth discovery was that I was unconsciously trying to heal my original childhood wounds with my mom through relationships with people like her.

I often fell in love quickly with men who were not capable of loving me back adequately. Therefore, I never felt loved and had recreated the familiar, chronic emptiness I sought to escape. Subconsciously, I had chosen these people to recreate the familiar feelings of childhood—the original wound from the mother-daughter relationship that mimicked rejection and cemented my belief that I am not good enough or lovable. It was as if I had been recycling the same relationship but with different people.

Once I became consciously aware of this pattern and realized how my past hurts played out in my present life, I needed to learn how to effectively relate to others and form healthy relationships. At that time, I began studying attachment theory and learned our personal attachment styles are developed in our first years of life—with our primary caregivers—and often stay with us into our future relationships. I discovered the varying attachment styles in *Attached: The New Science of Adult Attachment and How It Can Help You*

Find-and Keep Love by Amir Levine and Rachel S. F. Heller. Some of what I learned included anxious, avoidant, and secure styles. These classifications emerged from a study named the "strange situation test," conducted with babies ranging from nine to eighteen months old. The study involved having a child play with toys in an unfamiliar room with their mother present and one other observer who was overtly recording the test. The mother quietly left the room, unnoticed by the child. When the child realized the mother was absent, the way the child responded to her return gave evidence of the attachment they had with their mother. The behaviors exhibited by the children differed in three common ways, and became categorized into either an anxious, secure, or avoidant attachment style.[7] From other studies of mine, I realized there are more than these three styles, but for the sake of simplicity and how attachment styles relate to my recovery, I exhibited an anxious attachment style in most of my relationships.

The anxious profile describes an individual whose relationships consume a lot of their emotional energy, and they are overly sensitive to others' moods and actions, often taking the behaviors of their partner personally. This causes negative feelings to develop, which first begin with a lashing out, usually followed by regretting the outbursts. The person with an anxious style likes and wants to be very close with their partner, yet is preoccupied with a constant fear of rejection, thinking their partner does not wish the same.[8]

After a thoughtful and thorough examination following the book's guidelines and partner style assessment procedure, I determined my partners all had the same attachment style—avoidant. A person with an avoidant style is in stark contrast to those with the anxious style. They value their independence and feel uncomfortable with too much closeness. They fear being controlled and rarely open up emotionally, nor are they preoccupied with the fear of rejection.[9]

These two styles in a relationship seem to be a recipe for disaster because they foster "colliding intimacy needs." The needs of each person are in contrast to those of their partner and are the perfect combination to continually trigger each other's weaknesses and insecurities. The more the anxious person seeks closeness, the more the avoidant person seeks distance—emotionally and physically—creating a vicious cycle the book describes as the "anxious-avoidant trap." The anxious person is constantly feeling rejection, while the avoidant one is always running because they fear being controlled.[10] As a person with an anxious style, I often felt my relationships were at risk, never knowing if the person was going to stay or leave and never look back. This lack of security was familiar because my childhood and first attachments looked and felt identical. I had been abandoned, forgotten, rejected, unloved, and felt anxious in all my relationships, not knowing if this person was going to be there for me. This was all I knew, but relationships containing these two styles of attachment created extreme highs and lows for me—the "roller coaster effect"—which became a neurochemical addiction (serotonin, dopamine, oxytocin, norepinephrine).[11] Attaching to partners quickly in the beginning created intense emotions and a flood of chemicals that created a high. But with consistency and stability, the high fizzled, then boredom, anxiety and past trauma took over, and I was already pursuing the next relationship and the high that accompanied it. It was an addiction that had me on a desperate search for love but never staying long enough to allow myself to be loved.

Through the examination of my relationship history, I saw the self-fulfilling prophecy of my life's story: my fear of rejection/abandonment created an anxious attachment to others while believing I was not enough for them to stay.

These fears, thoughts, and beliefs spurred actions/behavior. Defense mechanisms then kicked in, and I went into survival and protection mode, acting out and sabotaging the relationship in various ways. Because all of this had happened unconsciously, the result was always the same, and I couldn't understand why. For a long time, I continued living in my chronic state of emptiness while repeating the same patterns.

I discovered this powerful truth: my anxious style can thrive if I partner with someone who has a secure attachment style, someone who can offer me reassurance (unlike those with an avoidant style, to whom I gravitated). In time, attachment styles can change. As I learned to feel secure in the relationship and tolerated the boredom because it meant it wasn't an addictive relationship, I then moved toward stability. By recognizing the red flags of avoidant-attachment styles or entitled schemas, I could avoid those people, change my anxious style, and break my addictive pattern.

6

DISCOVERING LEARNED FEARS—
ABANDONMENT WOUNDS

Fear is a question. What are you afraid of and why?
Our fears are a treasure house of self-knowledge
if we explore them.

—Marilyn French

L ife after trauma looks and feels different. You become preoccupied with mental warfare: worrying about the many potential threats you'll face each day. It can become too difficult to engage with people. For self-preservation, we avoid people and places, locking ourselves up in our invisible comfort bubble. Eventually, it becomes an ever-shrinking bubble of isolation.

The opposite of fear is trust. It can take a tremendous amount of courage to learn to trust. Especially if your trauma left you rejected by the people you had trusted the most—your family. Holding onto the trauma history of neglect, I was hypersensitive to perceived rejection, trying to avoid it at all costs. Fear became a navigation system throughout the journey of life, leaving me in a chronic state of hypervigilance. For a long time, the lack of awareness left me enslaved to my fears.

Coming to terms with my fear of rejection, I soon realized it was an abstract concept I couldn't easily put into words. Defining what rejection meant to me and what it looked like brought me to a profound revelation. Sensing rejection from my peers led to the dreaded and familiar feeling of abandonment as a child. At the core of BPD lies the fear and avoidance of abandonment.

My perception of rejection differed from others', and the slightest interaction or lack thereof could trigger feelings of loss. The fear of abandonment fueled my people-pleasing and chameleon-like behaviors, and I had hoped to receive love and acceptance in return for pleasing them. Lacking a solid identity of my own, I got my sense of self and self-worth from the people I served. Losing them meant I lost myself: the equivalent of a figurative death. This explained my thinking when a relationship ended: *The relationship is over; I might as well die.*

Although extreme, this was a common thought of mine— one that led me to an impulsive suicide attempt, which differed from the suicidality of a depressed person who thinks about and plans their exit. My suicidal thoughts often occurred after experiencing an intense feeling of abandonment—an intolerable sensation I had to escape.

Because my existence and sense of worth depended on others, losing someone meant I no longer felt validated. The physical and emotional pain of abandonment felt like death to me. Essentially, I placed my life in the hands of others.

FEAR OF LETTING OTHERS DOWN— MISPLACED GUILT AND RESPONSIBILITY

Growing up in an inconsistent environment, emotions had become messy. They often were a source of embarrassment, guilt, and shame. I had learned to act according to what I thought others wanted from me, which led me to further detach from my true self. Since I wasn't allowed to be a person and feel my emotions as a child, I lacked the ability to identify my feelings, didn't develop the skills needed to express them, and doubted what I felt. I also carried misplaced emotions—those that were not mine to own. For example, even if I had done nothing wrong, I felt a chronic sense of guilt, not realizing it was inappropriate or misplaced. This emotional response was rarely valid, yet I felt guilty simply for things like saying no, not doing things for others, having fun, and accepting a compliment.

Throughout my recovery, each time I worked on breaking away from an unhealthy pattern or an unhealthy person in my life, I felt this guilt. Even when the person was abusive or the pattern was harmful to me, I felt guilty, as if I had done something immoral. In part, this was the reason I stayed in abusive situations or continued similar harmful behavior patterns—the guilt associated with changing for my own betterment felt uncomfortable. This feeling contributed to making me an easy target for others to control.

When I let go of misplaced guilt and allowed people to carry their own guilt, my growth caused others to react harshly toward me. They were used to me being a certain way, so when I stopped doing what they expected, they acted as if they were trying to push me back into the mold of the person they knew—the one they needed me to be. It was like a dance, going back and forth, trying to get in step and in sync with this new dynamic. Sometimes, I lost people, which was extremely hard since it was their acceptance and love I had fought for all along. It was a high price for me to pay. The changes and letting go of this guilt came easier when I added value to myself.

I had been attending therapy with Dr. Vand for about a year when I found out I was pregnant with my son. The father of my child and I were a match of perfect flaws, reenacting together our familiar childhood trauma wounds and mismatched attachment styles. He had relapsed and became immersed in his heroin addiction, and I didn't want to be a single parent. It was during this time, the guilt of making changes and leaving him tormented me. I felt responsible for his addiction and as if I were abandoning him. For a long time, it was easier to live in the fantasy bubble of what I wanted things to be like—to see only the idea and the potential of the relationship, instead of the reality of how unhealthy it was. Dr. Vand often said, "You need to prick the bubble." I had to accept things for what they were and make a choice based on that truth.

MESSAGES FROM THE SUBCONSCIOUS— DREAM ANALYSIS

It is quite common among trauma survivors to have nightmares. While asleep, some trauma victims have terrifying dreams that mimic a traumatic event, while others have nightmares with a recurring theme that seems unrelated to their trauma. For many years, I suffered vivid, terrifying dreams that awakened me suddenly, sweating and in tears. These dreams had a recurring theme: I was drowning in a body of water. I hadn't formerly had a traumatic event that involved drowning; however, the nature of this dream was symbolic.

Upon the birth of my first child, dreams emerged of my newborn son dying. My child was floating in a body of water, drowning, and I was frantically trying to swim to him but could not reach him. I watched helplessly as he slipped away, disappearing into the depths. I looked around into the empty blue water with him nowhere in sight, and the pain of realizing he was gone jolted me awake. It was gut-wrenching. I awakened consumed with overwhelming heartache—unable to distinguish between my dream and reality—feeling deep sadness and grief only a mother knows. I discussed these disturbing dreams with my psychiatrist. Through the therapeutic process of dream analysis, I discovered the water symbolized deep and overwhelming emotions. My son was merely a representation of myself: the vulnerable, helpless childlike part of me. The one I couldn't save while enduring my traumatic childhood. Trapped in an abusive home, this deeply suppressed childhood memory had surfaced out of the depths of my subconscious into my awareness—it was the part of me that needed saving.

The next influential dream I encountered had also involved water. This time in a much different way. I was free falling out of the sky from an unknown high place and landed in the middle of a large ocean. Immersed in the deep, I looked through the seawater filled with creatures. Through my blurred and obscured vision, I saw a large, dark shadow coming my way. Sensing it was a large shark, in fear and panic, I swung my body in the opposite direction while covering my eyes and bracing for impact. Suddenly, I found myself on the shore, waking up on the sandy beach. As I looked around and felt unsure of what had happened, a man approached me. He explained I had been resurrected, much time had passed, and it was now the year 2051. Puzzled, I questioned him.

"I died? How did I die?"

"A shark bit you."

I looked down at my leg and saw a large, nasty scar across the entirety of my thigh. Upon awakening, I could not understand the meaning of this dream. But because of my previous dream analysis, I could analyze it. When I had the dream, I had been regularly and actively participating in therapy while also struggling in my relationship with my son's drug-addicted father. This left me torn between making the best decision about whether to stay with him or leave. It was a battle of heart versus head and with what I wanted versus what I knew was best. The high place from which I was falling in the dream possibly represented my current state of mind, which was becoming healthy in my recovery. However, plummeting through the sky symbolized the loss of my sense of control, perhaps the loss of control over my spouse's addiction and the consequences it brought to the relationship. I had a pattern of choosing and staying in toxic relationships, so I was, once again, engulfed by the sea of deep emotion that came with making the choice to break this pattern. The approaching shark was the symbolic representation of this negative pattern. My turning away and covering my eyes was an attempt to avoid my pain. I interpreted the resurrection portion of the dream as signifying my newfound awareness, knowing that going back to the relationship would be like going back to the shark, only to get bitten again.

PART 2
LETTING THE SCARS SPEAK

7

DISCOVERING DEFENSE MECHANISMS—SPLITTING AND SELF-INTERGRATION

She was like the moon—part of her was always hidden.

—Dia Reeves, *Bleeding Violet*

Developing borderline personality disorder meant I had a fragile and unstable identity sustained by a set of complex defense mechanisms. These mechanisms are the unconscious mental processes we all possess to avoid or deal with conflict, anxiety, and emotional distress. They develop early and become automatic, operating outside our awareness. If you had a psychologically healthy childhood, your mind uses these natural defenses productively to enhance daily functioning and protect you during life's challenges. For those of you coping with traumatic childhoods, these defenses might have helped you withstand a traumatic experience, but later, they can become destructive and dysfunctional. So, what helped your psyche survive during trauma, especially if that trauma was long-standing, can become habitual, remain long after you need it, and interfere with you living a healthy life and developing satisfying, wholesome relationships. Hence, experiencing any form of abuse and neglect in childhood can severely disrupt the way our brain forms and uses these defenses.

Growing up with constant feelings of terror and unpredictability, I developed a super-sensitivity to my environment and other people's emotions. Doing so helped me survive psychologically, but this chronic hypervigilance left me with my defenses always in the "on" position. Since my greatest wound was my mother's abandonment of me, lacking her love caused me to believe since even my mother could not love me, no one could. Holding this internalized message as truth, my unconscious defenses went into overdrive to avoid re-experiencing these painful feelings. Thus, I rejected others before they rejected me and sabotaged my relationships. I let no one get too close because I believed if they saw through my façade, they would run. The crumbs of affection I received from my shallow relationships caused me to want more. However, I was so busy running from people to prevent them from hurting me it was impossible to develop the closeness I craved and desperately needed.

Lacking a stable sense of self, the only way I could relate to people was on a superficial level, mirroring them by reflecting an image they could relate to and like. This chameleon behavior was a manifestation of another defense mechanism: *splitting*. Splitting refers to categorizing things in absolutes of either all good or all bad. People with borderline personality disorder see everything in only black or white, lacking comprehension of any nuances in (or even the existence of) grey areas. As infants, we all begin life seeing the world through the psychological lens of good or bad, hero or villain. As we mature psychologically, we integrate the grey areas into our perspective, develop a more complex lens, and understand good and bad can coexist. Trauma and neglect had stunted this growth in my perception, impairing how I saw myself and others. To avoid rejection, I needed to feel accepted while simultaneously protecting myself from getting hurt. My thinking and behaviors tried to make unconscious attempts to achieve both objectives. I aimed to perceive myself as all good, which I tried to achieve through perfectionism and people pleasing to gain acceptance, while my protective parts perceived me as all bad which sabotaged the relationship through reckless, impulsive, and self-destructive behavior.

My splitting defense also made me perceive others in this all-or-nothing fashion. If someone said or did something nice for me, my brain categorized them as all good. If someone said or did anything hurtful, I categorized them as all bad, even if they had been in the good category. My brain could not perceive the reality that good and bad can coexist in the same person or that it's possible to define a person's character based on most of their behavior over time, not on a single incident.

In an exercise during therapy, I drew a circle on a piece of paper to represent my personality. Within the circle, I wrote the many aspects of my personality—the things I liked and disliked about myself, good and bad. This exercise helped me discover I showed only limited facets of my personality with certain groups of people. I unconsciously chose aspects I had determined they would most readily accept, based on my observations of the group. If they approved that part of me, then I denied (to myself) even the existence of the rest of my personality. Instead of being a whole person—acknowledging and accepting all parts of me—I mentally cut off and exiled parts I deemed unacceptable to that group. Operating from this partial-self version of me, which changed from group to group, made my identity enmeshed and dependent on theirs.

Using another drawing, my psychiatrist illustrated my splitting with an image of two slightly overlapping circles;

one circle represented my "good" self, while the other was my "bad" self. The overlapping section in the middle represented my fear of rejection and was the "cut off barrier," illustrating where I was not allowing these two selves to blend into a cohesive whole. Upon further exploration, I realized my split-off part, which I labeled as my "Bad-Self," was the part representing all my painful childhood emotions—the ones I had worked hard to bury deep within. I could not acknowledge this part of me because it held the painful memories of *not being good enough* if I were less than perfect. Splitting became my defense to block out this psychological pain. To merge these separate selves, we explored and described how each fractured-self served me and found an appropriate name for each one: Good-Self was "Perfectionist Oriana;" Bad-Self was "Chaotic Oriana." Below is the drawing:

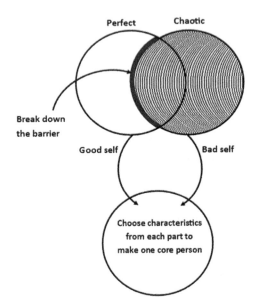

My life's history was one of chaos. The emotional distress and lack of control had me spinning like a tornado, destroying everything I touched. This chaotic self was a character I had grown into from the lies I believed about myself—one where I was the rejected, unloved problem child, becoming a villain in a story I hated. After disowning this chaotic-self, a new version was born: my perfectionist-self. This was the extreme opposite version, where my chaotic-self couldn't exist. The problem was, its inner story was still playing in the background of my mind. My perfectionism was the armor protecting those vulnerable parts, showing the world I had it together, showing them a different story. It provided me with a sense of control over the inner chaos and a place of belonging with my peers. However, feelings of belonging were always fleeting. I denied the rest of myself by keeping parts hidden, making it impossible for anyone to accept me fully.

Perfectionism—fueled by my belief I wasn't good enough and sustained by my fear of rejection—was a defense that wasn't maintainable; it set me up for failure and resulted from my cognitive distortion of all or nothing thinking. Perfectionism was my "all," and chaos was my "nothing." This perfect-self made my chaotic-self hold on to all our hurt and pain while ignoring "her" existence. Desperately wanting to be seen and heard, my chaotic-self became louder. When I experienced the inevitable fail of perfectionism, the part of me I had exiled (chaotic-self) re-emerged along with its painful emotions and took control, spiraling me into an episode of self-destructive behaviors for several days to extinguish my intolerable feelings.

For most of my twenties, I oscillated between these divergent selves. When I functioned from the perfect-self, I forgot about my chaotic-self, and when I became my chaotic-self, I forgot my perfect-self. They could not co-exist. That all-or-nothing lifestyle was a battle between my selves, and no one won.

When I actively operated as my chaotic-self, I could never be with one person, nor could I be the one to end a relationship. I was with one person while maintaining contact with others but keeping them at arm's length. As my psychiatrist described it, I had an enduring pattern of "leaving back doors open"—my "just in case doors." I could be extremely seductive and manipulative to keep people in their respective places and not lose anyone. This, of course, was another illusion because I had no one beyond a surface level. That never-ending, doomed search for love became my desperate way of life.

The primary goal of therapy was to become whole, which meant dropping the armor of the splitting defense mechanism. As my psychiatrist expressed: "Each Self worked against the other—imagine what they could do if they worked together!"

The next diagram she drew for me looked different from the previous ones. It displayed what a healthy-self looked like. She drew one circle with a fluid wall and opposing white and dark sides. It resembled a yin and yang symbol from ancient Chinese philosophy. *Yin* and *Yang* translated is "dark-bright," "negative-positive." It is a concept of dualism: two opposing forces being complementary and interdependent. I could apply this concept to my personality function. My two internal, opposing forces, good and bad, darkness and light, needed to work together to create harmony and balance. The image reveals a wholeness that comes when we accept all parts of us.

To practice self-acceptance, my psychiatrist did an exercise during our session. She presented small pieces of paper and said to write parts of myself I liked and didn't like. There were a handful of papers, but the two I remember clearly were the ones that said "addict" and "frightened child." I placed these slips of paper on the chairs around me and was told to approach each one and speak to them. Asking me to approach the frightened child part of me, Dr. Vand said, "What would you say to her?" I responded to this part of me with consoling words of comfort, love, and reassurance. Then, she pointed to the chair that said addict.

"What do you want to say to her?"

"I hate you!" I was angry and also yelled words of shame and disgust.

Then, Dr. Vand asked me why my expressions were different. After hearing my response, she said, "Don't you think the addict part of you deserves the same consolation as your frightened child? After all, they are the same person."

However obvious that statement might appear, it was a new truth that struck through my heart. My addict-self *is* the frightened child. These seemingly different parts were all one person. They all *needed love.* Being able to visualize each part of me in that chair and speak with them was a way to receive a love I had never felt before: self-love. That was what I lacked and so desperately needed in childhood—to receive the words of consolation I now gave myself: "I see you. I hear you. I understand you. I love you. You are safe with me." To heal into wholeness, love was much more productive than shame.

DISSOCIATION—DEPERSONALIZATION

The disconnection between one's mind and body are common among trauma survivors. To reconnect to my body, I had to face the trauma that had disconnected me. I began the work of healing the past with my family of origin, but we still had some other traumatic history to visit.

In a therapeutic session with Dr. Vand, I brought up memories (for the first time) of a past relationship with a man who was extremely abusive during my teen years. I had never disclosed the details of that relationship after I escaped, and I could hardly bear to speak about them in the session.

This relationship was one of terror, intimidation, and humiliation for me. I endured frequent physical attacks: getting smothered by pillows and plastic bags and intimidated by swords and a homemade flamethrower. He wanted to induce intense fear so I would not defy him. He burned my clothing, held me hostage in my home, drove at high speeds, and threatened to crash and kill us once as he threw me out of the moving vehicle. On other occasions, he forced me to have intercourse, and afterward, he hung me upside down by my ankles, thinking it would increase the odds of impregnating me. If I showed any weakness or cried, he held me down and bit my face, covering my mouth entirely with his as he pressed his teeth into my cheeks until he broke the skin.

As I recalled some of these events, they flooded me with memories and bodily sensations that suddenly left me feeling numb. This numbness had caused me to present to Dr. Vand as calm, but I later learned it was a trauma response of complete disconnection and separation of self, designed to protect me from the full psychological impact of what I had endured.

After this session, the numbness or calmness felt strange and robotic. I walked out of the building, pushed the button at the crosswalk, and looked down at my feet. While walking across the busy intersection, I felt as if my head were detached and floating somewhere above my body. I could see myself walking and hear my thoughts float by, noticing my legs carrying me across the street and the direction in which they were taking me. But I couldn't connect my thoughts to my body to change my course, and I continued walking past the lot where I parked my car and into the dingy local pub. At the bar, I ordered shooters to obliterate my existence, but I do not recall most of the night.

Feeling puzzled over the experience and ashamed of my actions, I shared this experience with Dr. Vand. While I described it, she interjected a term I was not yet familiar with, stating, "You disassociated." She also said I experienced depersonalization during that episode—a feeling of being detached from yourself as if you were watching yourself in a movie. I felt like an outside observer of my body and thoughts, with a loss of control over them. That was the first time I could fully recall experiencing the floating sensation or depersonalization. But the truth I had discovered was this disconnection and lack of control was a state I had been operating from for much of my life, and if I wanted to heal, I needed to stay grounded. Thereafter, Dr. Vand concluded sessions with grounding exercises to bring me back to the here and now.

EMOTIONAL AVOIDANCE

Because I had an enduring pattern of suppressing emotions, it eventually came out in other ways. Aside from splitting, I discovered another unconscious defense mechanism I used to bury my sadness: intellectualization. This mechanism is how we use *thinking* to avoid *feeling*—focusing on all the facts of a painful event instead of the emotions they carry.

This is an automatic avoidance of emotional discomfort that can lead us to dance around the emotion and focus on the factual conversation. I didn't know it then, but this happened after one of my greatest losses.

When I was about three months pregnant with my first child, I got a disturbing call from my mom. She said my eldest brother, Joel, was in the hospital, and we needed to get down there immediately. In her frantic voice, Mom explained Joel had overdosed, and the first responders were trying to resuscitate him.

When I arrived at the hospital, there was an eerie silence as I entered the room. Joel lay on the stretcher with a tube sticking out of his throat. My cousin, Greg, stood at the end of Joel's bed with his head resting on Joel's feet. The scene confused me, and I was unsure of what to conclude. I looked at Greg's girlfriend, who was by his side, and immediately, she pulled me in for a hug and began crying on my shoulder. I whispered in her ear, "Is he . . . ?" She nodded her head, but I was still in disbelief.

Initially, I had stared at my brother's lifeless body and concluded he was sleeping or unconscious. Unable to process his death, I asked Greg several questions about what had taken place and became persistent when he wouldn't engage in conversation. Without saying a word to me, Greg held my hand and walked me outside the hospital doors, but before he could speak, he vomited all over the ground. Even then, I continued throwing more questions at him while avoiding my grief, completely numb to the loss of my brother or Greg's pain. More people arrived at the hospital to offer goodbyes, and they were concerned about my unborn child. They said things to me like, "You can't cry because you'll stress out the baby." Feeling conflicted about my emotions over my brother and my unborn child, my efforts to suppress the tears turned into a deep moan that uncontrollably escaped from the pit of my belly, my body shaking as the groan vibrated through me. In retrospect, perhaps my unconscious intellectualization defense kicked in to protect me from the intensity of my grief and protect my unborn child from prenatal harm.

Sigmund Freud, the neurologist who invented psychoanalysis, believed memories have both conscious and unconscious aspects, and intellectualization allows for the conscious analysis of traumatic events without provoking anxiety. For three years after my brother's death, I rarely cried when I recalled that memory. Instead, I focused on the facts of his life, his health, his friends, details of the event that had led to his death, such as how long it took to get him to the hospital and how long he was without oxygen. Addiction and overdose prevention consumed my attention as I followed the statistics and researched the topic. I even received training to administer naloxone injections (an opioid overdose reversal medicine) and trained others to recognize the signs of an overdose and how to administer a naloxone injection.

Although there are some positives to intellectualization, which was true for me, the downside was it prevented me from dealing with my grief. I hadn't allowed myself the chance to sit with it and feel the significant loss it was for me and my son, who would never know his uncle. Because intellectualization is unconscious, I didn't realize all my efforts to help prevent addiction were due to a defense mechanism.

One evening about three years after my loss, I was out with a friend and had consumed a few casual drinks when, suddenly and without warning, it was as though a switch went off in my brain, and I completely broke down in uncontrollable tears. I didn't know why I was crying. When I returned home, I went to sleep, but in the early hours of the morning, the sound of my wailing awakened me. The realization struck me, and I cried out, "Joel!" I finally *felt* the loss. It was then clear why I was crying, and I realized my efforts to remain emotionally strong and pro-active were also a form of emotional avoidance.

8

DISCOVERING AND
BEFRIENDING EMOTIONS

Feel it. The thing you don't want to feel. Feel it. And be free."

—Nayirrah Waheed

Think of visiting your emotions as an intrapersonal meet and greet. You travel inward to meet the emotion, then you greet it with a hospitable welcome. For a person who has experienced trauma or neglect growing up, this comes neither naturally nor easily. So, support and practice with this encounter are necessary for healing.

I always found drawings helpful for understanding how things work. Visualizing through illustrations puts a picture in my mind's eye of what is happening inside me. The imagery used in my therapy likened my painful emotions to the current of a river. A river is continuously flowing and has naturally occurring rough spots, undercurrents, and calm spots. It is easy to imagine the difficulty in swimming against the current of a river and the risks of being swept away and pulled under. Waters like these mirror exactly how tumultuous and overwhelming emotions can be, producing the sensation of drowning. When you resist your emotions, it is like blocking the flow of the current—you are swimming upstream, and eventually, you will tire out and be swept under.

In my therapeutic work dealing with my avoidance of emotions, I pictured the avoidance as a dam built across the river, blocking its flow. As I visualized this figurative dam, I pictured the water intensifying in pressure, gradually rising and spilling over the wall. The pounding force of the water chipped away at the dam until I experienced its inevitable collapse. This emotional river felt as if my insides were trying to escape me. My dam of avoidance could no longer hold against the pressure—it was intolerable. My fight to avoid feelings collapsed under the pressure and swept me away in the rapids of self-destructive behaviors. The illustration of the dam was symbolic of the pattern I had created to ignore and avoid experiencing my emotions. The emotions increased in intensity and were too painful to face, which led me down the path of self-medicating through binge-drinking, drugging, and reckless behavior.

With the support of my psychiatrist, I was guided through grounding exercises where I connected with my body and inner experiences. This involved noticing how the emotions *live* within my body and learning to tolerate them. I sat in a chair with my feet planted firmly on the ground, hands placed on the arms of the chair, posture straight but comfortable, and my eyes gently closed. I relaxed my body by breathing—in the nose for four counts and out the mouth for four counts—and felt fully present and calm. At the doctor's request, I described all the physical symptoms I felt in my body. They included:

- A sore lump sensation in my throat.
- A tightness in my diaphragm.
- A tension in my lower back and neck.

"Now, put that physical pain into emotion; give it a name," she said.

"Sadness." I felt it instantly, and my reply was soft. Tears started streaming down my face, and I tried to wipe them away.

"Stop wiping your tears away. Stop fighting it."

Feelings of embarrassment and irritability washed over me and, suddenly, I became numb, disconnected, and felt nothing at all. I retreated to my old pattern of disconnecting when feelings became too much. This didn't mean the exercise wasn't a success. In fact, at that moment of a mind-body connection, I allowed myself to feel the sadness and noticed where my body held on to it. Those few tears were my body's way of releasing the emotion and physical tension, which enabled that river to flow freely. My participation in and practice of these exercises helped me expand my window of tolerance for difficult emotions.

I opened my eyes.

"Did you survive?" Dr. Vand asked.

"Yeah."

"Was it as intense and scary as you thought?"

"No, but I don't know why I feel sad."

"A feeling is a feeling—it's to be felt, not something to be solved or fixed."

She explained each time I had practiced this, it was like letting a stone out of the dam and relieving some pressure.

PRACTICING SELF-AWARENESS AND ALONENESS

Self-awareness was not a gift I possessed for most of my life, so developing my self-awareness was like a muscle I continuously needed to strengthen by making it a regular practice. Being self-aware meant knowing what my needs and wants were and how to meet them for myself. At the early stage of my recovery, if you had asked me what my needs or wants were, I would not have had the answer. I specifically remember when this question dumbfounded me. I was in a therapy session, feeling deep distress as I discussed an upcoming event. I was frantically explaining what all my friends wanted me to do or needed from me, and Dr. Vand interrupted me.

"I don't want to hear what your friends want. What do *you* want?"

"I don't understand the question," I said.

I had never thought about what *I* wanted. *What if my wants cause someone to dislike me and reject me?* I remember feeling confused and even horror at the thought of what I wanted; that option had never crossed my mind. Being so far removed from myself, I could not come up with an answer to her question, but I deeply pondered it after I left the session.

What do I want? What do *I want? Why have I never looked at this question in this way before?* I had become so attuned to serving others and out of tune with myself that I never developed an awareness of my needs or how to receive what I wanted. To obtain self-knowledge and understanding, I needed to connect with the emotional parts of me I avoided. Knowing my wants and needs, I discovered, was interconnected with my deep emotions, which made it so difficult for me for many years.

In some countries, they call borderline personality disorder emotionally unstable personality disorder (EUPD). This other title puts greater emphasis on the difficulty of regulating emotions effectively. In line with this, it often felt as if my emotions happened *to* me without the ability to feel or choose how to respond. Emotions felt too big, too overwhelming, and too intense. Living with this illness makes the minor inconveniences of life feel like too much. There seemed to be no space between my emotions and reactions—I had no choice in it.

Illness aside, as part of my personality, I feel emotions deeply—my own and others'. My empathy for others is as strong as any of my other emotions. However, there are many "super-feelers" and deep empaths who, unlike me, can manage their emotions effectively and maintain their self-care. The difference between us is I never learned how to self-regulate in my childhood. Because of the emotional neglect and chronic invalidation by my caregivers during childhood, I never learned how to first identify, then express my emotions, so I could not regulate them in healthy ways. By avoiding the emotions that threatened to overwhelm me, the power they held over me became stronger. My higher-than-normal emotional reactivity, coupled with my inability to regulate my emotions, caused me to avoid any feelings.

It is a deadly combination to be a super-feeler who refuses to feel her own emotions. Not only had I learned to suppress and avoid emotion, but I had also developed a host of maladaptive coping strategies and defense mechanisms to help me escape them. That always raised the question for me: Do I (someone with a borderline personality disorder) have stronger emotional feelings than others, or do my emotions seem stronger to me because I've suppressed them? Or is it a combination of both? Whatever the case, I have learned if I accept and feel my emotions, it reduces both their intensity and the strength of their power over me. The problem is, unlike an emotionally healthy person who naturally and automatically feels and addresses their emotions, I lacked this automatic ability. I had to schedule the time to feel like I had done in therapy. I needed to check in with myself and do some emotional inventory.

To strengthen my emotional intelligence (EQ), I noticed the physical sensations in my body, such as back pain, heartburn, a tight chest, or a headache. I also noted physical behaviors I used to cope with the emotions (e.g., clenching my jaw or skin picking). To be vigilant about catching my emotional coping strategies, I practiced pausing throughout the day to *notice* these cues, then had an internal dialogue. Here are some examples:

"Okay, I see I am doing _____." (Identify the behavior.)

"I notice my body feels _____." (Identify physical sensations/tensions.)

"I have been thinking/saying to myself _____." (Identify thoughts.)

"What emotion am I feeling/suppressing?" _____. (Name the authentic emotion.)

Then, allow yourself to feel it. Sit with it.

As I attempt to resolve whether these thoughts are self-regulating or dysregulating, I determine how they are contributing to this emotional/behavioral chain:

thoughts -> feelings -> actions.

Most of the time, my inner narrative is playing faintly in the background—thoughts of a dysregulating nature—a negative theme of criticism, judgments, self-doubt, worry, and fear. These thoughts create distressing emotions that trigger my stress response, then the coping behaviors appear.

Once I have discovered the thoughts, their nature, and the presenting physiological symptoms, to lessen and relieve my distress, I examine whether the thoughts are true. Usually, they're not, but even if the thought is true (e.g., if I'm feeling legitimate guilt or remorse over something I've done), I ask myself a question: can I change my perception of it so it doesn't become debilitating? In almost every situation, I can. Sometimes, the relief is not immediate, but I can get onto the right path—lowering the intensity of the emotion while increasing my self-awareness.

To be self-aware means to be mindful—aware of the present moment. Practicing mindfulness is difficult when you've spent a lifetime trying to escape the moment. I was often the opposite: mind full—full or occupied with everything else but the present.

To continue exercising my self-awareness and emotional regulation, Dr. Vand had referred me to another avenue of therapy: Dialectical Behavior Therapy (DBT). DBT is a specific type of cognitive-behavior psychotherapy that incorporates the Buddhist practices of acceptance and mindfulness. An American psychologist, Marsha Linehan, developed DBT in the late 1980s specifically to treat borderline personality disorder, although it has proven helpful for other disorders. Dialectic is the term used to convey this concept: two things that appear opposite can be both true at the same time. This underlies the notion we accept ourselves as we are yet also realize we need to change. They teach DBT as a series of skills through four main modules, including mindfulness, distress tolerance, emotion regulation, and interpersonal effectiveness.

In the first three months of group therapy, using DBT, I did not apply myself much. Rarely could I bring myself to share with the group what I wrote in my journal over the weekends. This was because of my feelings of utter shame and humiliation about my actions most of the time. I listened to others share during the morning check-in. One person graphically described her self-inflicted wounds and how her teenage daughter was mimicking her and cutting too. Another group member was crying in deep regret at having impulsively hacked off all her hair, while another member regularly stormed in and out of the room because she was constantly in conflict with the group facilitators (usually when they told her time for sharing was up, and they had to move on).

I had been feeling horrified about my experience over the previous weekend and somehow mustered up the courage to share. I told the group I had been drinking on a party bus with friends, and I also consumed GHB (Gamma-hydroxybutyrate), which resulted in me losing consciousness. I described waking up in one of my male friend's arms and realized he was carrying me toward the door. The bus door opened, and he threw me outside—where I landed face down on the wet cement—leaving me behind. It was late, dark, cold, and raining, but I was hot with anger. As I watched the bus disappear into the distance, I resolved to go to the local bar, drink some shooters, walk to the bridge, and throw myself off it. *I'll show them how much they hurt me. I'll make them regret this!*

While walking, a homeless man approached me, noticing I was soaking wet and without a coat, and he offered me his. He asked me where I was going. Without revealing my purpose, I told him I was walking to the bridge, and he offered to walk with me. After our conversation and a quick stop at a gas station, we parted ways at the bottom of the bridge. Then, my phone rang. It was my FP (favorite person), Tanya. I explained to her what happened and confessed I was near the bridge (I later learned she drove down there but couldn't find me). As I walked along the walkway at the side of the bridge, I made it to the very peak, grabbed the railing, and looked over the edge. It was pitch black.

Suddenly, out of the corner of my eye, I saw red and blue flashing lights and two police officers, one male and one female, approaching me. I ran, but one officer soon caught and attempted to restrain me. After wrestling on the ground for a few minutes, my top came down, exposing my breasts. Embarrassment washed over me, and I surrendered, asking them to help me with my shirt as they assisted me into their vehicle.

The male officer escorted me into the hospital, where we waited for a psychiatric evaluation. He accompanied me in the waiting room for about an hour. "Why would you want to do such a thing?" he asked. Later, he chuckled and said, "You put up quite a good fight; you're much stronger than you look." Within that hour, his company, sincerity, and compassion helped me feel better—I felt someone cared.

I shared this story in my DBT group because I didn't know what would have happened if the police hadn't arrived when they did. Also, I wondered if I hadn't revealed to Tanya I was near a bridge, would I have followed through? Knowing this was too serious to keep secret, I shared my experience, hoping to answer these questions:

- What would it have proven if I were successful in my attempt?
- Would it have taught my male friend a lesson?
- Would it have hurt him as I hurt?
- Was teaching him a lesson worth the price of my life?

This step in vulnerability and self-exploration was the beginning of applying the DBT skills and the critical skill of mindfulness. I quickly learned for DBT to work, I had to work; I had to apply myself fully, day after day, and skill after skill.

Being alone was another extremely challenging endeavor. When alone, I couldn't ignore my thoughts. I needed time to be alone with myself to practice mindfulness. One trait of BPD is *frantic efforts to avoid being alone*, and frantic I was. Being alone with my thoughts and feelings produced an emptiness that threatened my very existence and often left me agitated and pacing. My sense of self and identity had always been tenuous, based on the input and evaluation of others, so being alone left me without that crutch and meant I must confront the feelings I did not want to face. Since I had avoided being alone at all costs, recovery meant I had to practice being alone—a scary proposition. My fear was legitimate, which Dr. Vand expressed accurately, "You are used to coping with alcohol and people; now, you're facing the world alone." I practiced facing my fear by spending short periods alone while engaging in activities and using sensory tools designed to help me cope as thoughts and feelings arose.

My nervous energy ramped up, I discovered, while sitting or resting because my perfectionism caused me to think about the things I should have been doing instead. Mindfulness meant to notice these thoughts without judging them or adding emotion—to observe the thought, let it go, and continue my practice. To be self-aware, you must be mindful and fully present in your aloneness. This practice helps us to stop viewing our thoughts and emotions as feared enemies but as trusted friends instead—ones who will show us our truth.

9

TRAUMA IN THE BODY

*In order to change, people need to become aware of their
sensations and the way that their bodies interact with
the world around them. Physical self-awareness is
the first step in releasing the tyranny of the past.*

—Dr. Bessel Van Der Kolk, *The Body Keeps the Score*

The belief that we can hold trauma captive in our body is gaining a more common understanding. This stored trauma that stays alive in our body presents itself through physical sensations, aches, pains, and other physical illnesses. I learned a valuable truth about trauma: trauma is *not only the event* we suffered, but it is also the energetic residue left in our nervous system from the traumatic event. It is the inability of the nervous system to deactivate *after* the event—to return to baseline and feel internal security. Trauma gets stored in the body or becomes frozen because our nervous system has been flooded, leaving us in a state of constant high alert if no resources are available to find safety. As a result, the person remains physically and psychologically traumatized, and their nervous system can retraumatize them after the event is over.

Many people have experienced traumatic situations and have received love, comfort, and understanding afterward—they felt safe again; therefore, their nervous system could release that traumatic energy and return back to its regulated (calm) state within the autonomic nervous system (often after therapy). Feeling safe, their body knew the event was over—the flight, fight, freeze, and shutdown response no longer needed to stay activated to protect and help them survive. For many people, one specific experience caused their trauma, such as what soldiers endured in the battlefield or others suffered from being in a car accident. Those people may develop post-traumatic stress disorder (PTSD), and they're condemned to relive that same event repeatedly (sometimes for decades) through flashbacks, physical, sensory, and emotional feelings etched into their nervous systems. I, however, did not fully experience this form of trauma-recurrence. Emotional flashbacks suddenly hijacked me with intense feelings of dread, despair, panic, and helplessness. I responded to them by running (flight response) or self-numbing behaviors.

In contrast to those with PTSD from a single trauma, I had a lifetime pattern of interpersonal trauma: events where others harm the victim, such as child abuse and sexual abuse. My interpersonal trauma comprised a long and pervasive history of caregiver relationships lacking in stability, reciprocity, emotional-attunement, and safety. It involved repeated emotional abuse, neglect, and assaults during the earlier and most critical developmental years of my life. This trauma is complex and can be difficult to diagnose and treat. Victims are often said to have a complex form of PTSD, which can have overlapping symptoms with BPD. My trauma led me to become miss-attuned and disconnected with myself, my wants, needs, values, and even my physical body.

REPARENTING THE INNER CHILD

I hid parts of myself and became only an outer shell, portraying versions of myself I thought others could love and accept. One night, I was reminded of this when I went to a bar with a friend. Having some therapy under my belt helped me cope with what happened next. Jewel, a former friend with whom I had long been estranged, entered the bar, and I immediately felt apprehensive. I tried to avoid eye contact, but upon seeing me, she approached and was relentless in her questions.

"Are you mad at me?" she asked.

"No! I'm just hurt." I had been struggling to speak for myself and ignored her question at first, but she badgered me into giving her an answer. My other friend tried to defend me, which appeared to infuriate Jewel.

"And that's what I hate about you: you have no personality!"

Jewel's statement pierced through my very soul. Painfully, she was right. I portrayed who I thought others wanted me to be but never lived my true self. Jewel probably wanted me to finally say, "YES! I am angry" to stand up for myself and speak my truth. But I choked in the face of conflict and let my friend speak on my behalf. *What does she mean, I have no personality? I have many!* The tone of my thoughts was joking at first, but it was true: I was a chameleon and could be anyone I needed to be in that moment—except myself. I didn't have a self. I lived a lie because I was disconnected from my truth.

Sometimes, people could view my behavior as manipulative, but from a psychological perspective, I now understand they are my survival strategies when I have emotions and thoughts that threaten to annihilate me.

Hiding these certain exiled parts of myself was extremely difficult to ignore when I became emotionally and physically triggered. The emotional flashbacks from PTSD produced surges of intense feelings and urges to escape, which often drove me into self-destructive behaviors. Becoming aware of my triggers helped acquaint me with the parts of myself I didn't acknowledge. When my triggers did not sweep me away, my awareness of them served as an invitation to meet myself.

The word "trigger" can hold a negative tone, but I've come to learn I don't need to judge my triggers as bad, even though they may *feel* bad. When we use the word "bad" (even in our thoughts), we attach judgment to our feelings, which can make us feel worse. These triggered feelings are just sensations. To remain neutral and unafraid of them, I view triggers as my inner child delivering a message—don't shoot the messenger! My triggers reveal a secret self, one that was hidden from me by my psyche and lived on within me, constantly on the search for safety. I learned to think of this trigger as a real-life time travel, bringing me back in time to an unresolved trauma—here is the opportunity to meet, reparent, and heal this part of me.

If childhood experiences include being parented by those ill-equipped to meet the fundamental needs of a child, those experiences can create a longing and intense craving for nurture. For survivors of developmental trauma, the need may have never been met, or met inconsistently from their family of origin. But they may never receive it in the way they need and deserve. Resisting this truth and trying to squeeze nurturing from a neglectful parent leads to recurring disappointment which ever-deepens childhood wounds. Sometimes, I still feel like a little girl with an unquenchable craving for a loving, nurturing parent—to be held, caressed, comforted, even admired. To remedy such a feeling, I try to fulfill my need through other healthy sources and accept what love and nurturing I can receive from my parents, knowing it is the best they can give.

The younger, unloved, and traumatized parts of us continue to live within, stored as body memory—our nervous system hasn't forgotten, and our inner child's belief system is still operating. When we experience a trigger, it is in effect, the inner, younger self recalling what happened in the past and is striving to protect us from danger and the pain of re-experiencing it. The parental/caregiver relationship lacking in approval, security, validation, and love can lead us down a path of self-hate and self-numbing. To recover, we need the opposite: self-love and self-awareness. Being aware of these younger parts then enables us to meet them with love.

Upon feeling triggered, my former pattern would be to either ignore or to be unaware of what was happening and why, with my sole focus on numbing the inner emotional discomfort and physical sensations. This pattern is the equivalent of a person, perhaps a child, tugging at your leg and asking for your help, only to have you turn your back toward them. As children experiencing big emotions, we look to our caregivers to provide us the support in regulating our distress through parental attunement. Attunement happens when the parent observes the cues from the child's behaviors, reflects them to the child, and then responds accordingly with their focused energy—tuning-in to their child's experience, validating it, and fulfilling the child's need of co-regulation. It is not the parent joining in the emotional storm by getting angry, dismissing, or being unavailable but happens through accurate attuning and modeling ways to find calm—bringing their nervous system down to baseline—i.e., into a regulated, calm, relaxed state. As a result, the child feels seen, heard, understood, and safe. This co-regulation builds resiliency for the many threats children face and gives them the knowledge to grow into an adult with the skills to self-regulate.

A trigger is a form of nervous-system dysregulation. It is an old wound resurfacing to communicate the threat of danger—our past telling us *we've been here before, and something bad happened.* How does this happen? Dr. Stephan W. Porges coined the term neuroception, which he described as a subconscious system in the primitive part of the brain, designed to detect threats and safety of people and places.[12] Our neuroception is based on our experience. It is always on the look-out, unconsciously scanning our environment for threats toward our physical and emotional wellbeing. When past trauma is a factor, our perception of danger is changed, and we may have triggers that are false alarms. Even if they are false, your body can't distinguish the difference, and your autonomic nervous system (ANS) responds accordingly— secreting stress hormones and soon bodily sensations flood you with the urge to either fight, run, freeze or shut down. It can be extremely frustrating and exhausting to live with a nervous system that is frequently revving on high alert with little to no rest between. This is not our fault. Our autonomic nervous system has served us well, and those protective parts have worked hard to aid us in surviving former traumatic experiences. When we haven't received parenting with the attunement and co-regulation needed to find safety, or our parents/caregivers were the sources of our dysregulation, as adults, we will need the skill to reparent those younger parts when they surface.

Reparenting involves releasing the energy of our ANS, reducing the physical sensations, and returning to calm—an internal place of safety. A self-parenting practice I found helpful to regulate the nervous system in this way is found in Somatic Experiencing (SE), developed by Dr. Peter Levine.[13] Instead of ignoring this remnant of the younger self within (i.e., the messenger), this practice will help a trauma victim notice their triggering physical sensations and practice doing what a loving parent would do: tune-in to the experience. Tuning in requires the person to notice, listen, and (if possible) identify the age of their inner child. They then validate and accept their experience while connecting with their body— recalling a time they felt safe, breathing deeply and slowly to shift those bodily sensations, and showing themselves what a calm and safe state feels like. They use touch with this practice by placing their hands on the areas they feel the physical sensations, perhaps on their chest and over their heart, while expressing gratitude for every beat it takes. It is best to try this with the guidance of an experienced SE practitioner. With severely traumatized individuals who experience intense flashbacks, they must be with a skilled therapist who can support them to stay grounded and in a state of safety, while accessing these former traumatic experiences, so they will not be retraumatized. As I suggested before, the trigger is like time travelling—it takes us back to that moment, and we can lose our sense of time, no longer being aware we are in the present. So, the goal with this practice is to integrate the past into the grand scheme of our life's timeline, not to relive it but to resolve it.

NEUROFEEDBACK

Tackling my emotional flashbacks was a challenge. Even after having been in recovery for a while and becoming much more stable, intense and overwhelming feelings flooded me and caused me to run from my house into my vehicle and drive aimlessly. The intensity of these feelings was so strong I sometimes pulled over at a random destination (e.g., an empty parking lot) and harmed myself—sometimes pulling my hair, slapping or punching myself, screaming, and wailing hysterically. I did not know why this happened or even where these compulsions came from. They came on suddenly and without warning, and I just had to endure them until they passed.

I discovered neurofeedback was helpful for these episodes—a self-control brain training for people who seem neurologically stuck.[14] This treatment is done with electroencephalography (EEG), a brain monitoring method to record electrical activity in the brain. Neurofeedback measures your brain waves, which reveal your existing brain functions and trains you to keep regulated and calmer patterns through biofeedback. It does so by sending audio and visual rewards (positive reinforcement) to your brain when you are calmer, which helps you maintain this calmer state.

I began with a few treatments and noticed I felt noticeably calmer after the session. We scanned my brain activity before and after to compare the readings. There was significant improvement, with my brain looking more integrated—both sides of the brain working together. However, there was a particular brain wave that remained constant—it wouldn't budge. The trauma therapist said it was in the mental processing part of my brain and was most likely where my trauma resided. He suggested I return for a neurofeedback session, followed by a structured session where we would use a technique called Trauma Indecent Reduction (TIR). TIR involves revisiting the trauma and facing it head-on in a safe environment. The therapist offered reassurance, stating, "Don't worry—I won't let you leave here bleeding."

To prepare for the TIR, I completed a session of neurofeedback for 30 minutes, bringing my wavelength to a calmer state. Then, the trauma specialist asked me to choose a traumatic event. Once I had picked the event, the therapist asked me to tell it like a story, notice how I was feeling, and number its emotional intensity on a scale from zero to ten (ten being the highest intensity and zero representing the absence of emotional intensity). Then, I had to repeat it a second time mentally, silently playing the event in my mind, and when I was done, I had to discuss what I had felt, seen, heard, observed, and rate my emotional intensity. We did this several times until my emotional intensity was at a one or zero on the scale.

I chose the incident mentioned in earlier chapters when I was a child and my mother chased me with a knife. While repeating the story, revisiting it in my mind, I noticed different things each time. About halfway through the hour session, I experienced a full-body sensation, like a wave of racing hot blood pumping through me, causing me to tingle and feel a sense of dread and panic, which was closely followed by the urge to get up and run. It was that same feeling I experienced when I had an emotional flashback, causing me to flee the house or self-harm. I had finally made the connection and identified the original trauma, its energetic residue stuck in my system. Without acting on the urge and fleeing the room, I could notice the feeling and endure it, going through the story again and again. After each repetition, I expressed my observations and again chose a number. As we repeated this exercise, it overwhelmed me less, and after an hour of retelling this story and narrating it as an observer, I rated my emotional intensity at number one on the scale. I felt no emotion attached to the story anymore; it was only an event, and I could leave it where it belonged—in the past.

The therapist further explained: while it might feel a little strange at first that this traumatic event no longer upset me in the same way (because it might feel like it should), squarely facing it and the gentle, energetic nudging of neurofeedback had finally processed the traumatic memory and removed the overwhelming emotion attached to it. It has been a few years since this session, and I have yet to reencounter this type of flashback.

CHRONIC PAIN AND TRAUMA—BOTTOM-UP HEALING

Most of my healing involved strengthening my cognitive awareness of my thoughts, feelings, and beliefs so I could understand my experiences and make sense of my world. They call this a top-to-bottom approach. But my body, through its visceral discomfort and chronic back pain, was telling me something my mind couldn't resolve on its own.

Since trauma is the memory or imprint of a nervous system response left unresolved, the protective aspects of the autonomic nervous system remained active: fight, flight, freeze, or shut-down responses are continuously working and exhausting the entire system. Being in this constant state of high alert, other functions of the entire organism do not function properly, causing a host of physical problems and illnesses. Although my mind understood the past is behind me, my body was still in a physical state of self-protection.

Since adolescence, I had been plagued with chronic back pain. By my twenties, I was hospitalized due to acute, intense lower back pain preventing me from walking. The hospital doctors diagnosed me with sciatica and piriformis syndrome, and an MRI showed a bulged L4 in my spine. They put me on a waitlist for a guided ultrasound to determine if I had an SI joint dysfunction. I took a variety of medications to manage my pain and decrease my migraines and acid reflux. To improve my condition, I tried many services, such as chiropractic with traction, physiotherapy, and massage therapy. One sports massage therapist made a discovery that later changed my life. As he applied pressure to my belly down to the deeper layers of my core muscle, the pain became so intense that I trembled, sweat, and felt dread and panic. He educated me about the muscle he released—the psoas (pronounced so-as), which is referred to as "the muscle of the soul."

"The psoas is a primal messenger of the central nervous system. It is much more than simply a muscle, it can be perceived as the guardian or spokes-person of Dan Tien, Hara, or what is commonly referred as to your 'gut intuition.' "[15]

The massage therapist found this was where I held my tension. This large muscle group connects our upper and lower body, controlling posture and much of our movement and more. It is attached to our diaphragm, which controls our breath. The psoas and the diaphragm work together in responding to threats or when our survival is at stake. When the ANS activates and we are in a state of fight or flight, it signals the psoas muscle to shorten, thus tightening the diaphragm resulting in short, shallow breaths.

Communication between our mind and body is bi-directional—goes both ways (mind to body and body to mind)—they create a feedback loop. The stored trauma held in my muscle memory left me with a chronically tight or shortened psoas muscle, which signaled my nervous system there was danger. No matter how much my mind understood there was no present danger, my body was not responding and releasing.

The chronic shortening of the lower part of this muscle caused a condition called hyperlordosis (an increased C-shape in the lower back), and the tight upper psoas created tension in the solar plexus, pushing my diaphragm forward and contributing to acid reflux. I lived in a chronic state of fight and flight with internal discomfort and pain. Massage therapy helped, but the relief was short-lived. To show (not tell) my body I was safe, I needed something I could put into practice daily. This is called a bottom-up approach to releasing trauma.

In my search for such an approach, I discovered specific exercises called TRE: Tension and Trauma Releasing Exercises created by Dr. David Berceli.[16] These exercises are designed to safely activate the body's natural reflex mechanism of shaking/vibrating to release stress, tension, and trauma. I used specific exercises and postures designed to fatigue my psoas muscle. Afterward, I lay on the floor in a constructive rest position—flat on my back with my knees bent—this is the resting pose for the psoas muscle. In this position, I experienced an involuntary shaking for several minutes, as my body naturally cleansed itself of the stored tension.

Discomfort can be a great teacher if you listen to its message—this type of body intelligence (BQ) reflects how you hold your experiences in your body so you can respond accordingly.[17] Having a healthy relationship with my body enabled me to self-regulate and become less dependent on external regulation and numbing.

PART 3
LIVING YOUR TRUTH

10

TAKING BACK POWER

Pain is inevitable. Suffering is optional.

—Haruki Murkami

When trying to heal from the hurts of our past, we often look for someone to take responsibility, either blaming others or ourselves. We may feel intense urges to confront the person who has harmed us and to seek validation for our pain. Feelings of helplessness can quickly choke out this urge and the void left from not having this satisfaction, can feel like an overwhelming sense of powerlessness, perhaps similar to what was felt while enduring our trauma—being unable to stop it. When being bullied by our family members—those we expect to protect us—it becomes a type of powerlessness that threatens to annihilate the ability to have control over our life.

A child's vulnerability leaves them at the mercy of the adults and abusers in their life. As a grown woman with children of my own, I longed for the courage to confront my abusive mother, but as soon as my urge to confront her arose, childlike feelings of powerlessness extinguished it. This familiar power struggle was the battlefield of my home. These automatic, knee-jerk feelings had been engraved on my inner being. The feelings of powerlessness and helplessness had become a dominant theme in my interactions with others for much of my life. I began therapy without a clue of what control and power were since much of my life circumstances hadn't allowed me to develop this type of self-agency. Often overwhelmed by crushing feelings of learned powerlessness, the expression of defeat and "I don't know how" was a theme that surfaced in therapy sessions—one that had become a false mantra I used to surrender. This mantra kept me in the fixed cycle of helplessness and powerlessness which resulted in me being at the mercy of others' demands. I wanted to overcome this self-defeating passivity, but I didn't know how to change it. I didn't believe I could ever speak out and live my truth—even in the simplest interactions. Once I had a deeper understanding of where and why this learned powerlessness began, my psychiatrist conducted role-playing exercises with me, and I practiced expressing myself to strengthen my sense of autonomy. These exercises also gave me the vocabulary to articulate my feelings in a safe environment—without fear of backlash and compulsive submission.

Learning to assert myself included the dreadful feelings that came with saying *no*, those feelings made me wonder. *Why did this simple word terrify me so much? Why did it bring me intense physical discomfort to say no to someone?* Saying yes was reflexive—without thinking much about what I wanted, I'd agree. This reflex to agree with others was a trauma response I've come to know as *fawning*. It is a people-pleasing response to diffuse conflict and earn others' approval to feel more secure. What it became was a quick route to building resentment. Saying *yes* to more things than I could carry became extremely burdensome. No matter what anyone asked of me, I believed I *had* to accommodate.

This topic arose in a therapy session, and my psychiatrist addressed it.

"Has anyone ever said no to you?"

"Yes, just the other day I invited a friend to go for coffee, and she said no; she wasn't able to."

"How did it feel?"

"It felt fine. I understood; we can always reschedule."

This simple reflection made me see how elementary my conditioning was. I realized everyone must say no sometimes; it's just a part of life. Often, I unconsciously projected my feelings of rejection onto others, believing if I said no, they would feel rejected, and I'd lose them forever. Never having asserted my voice or opinion, saying no proved to be a substantial challenge. My past taught me it wasn't safe to question or deny a request. I just did as I was told to stay safe, avoid rejection, and gain love and a feeling of worthiness.

Since fawning was part of my conditioning throughout my developmental years, I needed to recondition myself. The feelings of rejection are mine, and I could no longer assume other people felt the same. The only way to make a change and break away from the conditioning was to practice something different, to assert myself.

My therapist suggested I replace the word "no" with a statement or question that would buy me more time. Instead of a yes or no answer, I could say something as simple as "can I have more time to think about it and get back to you?" This would give me the time to think over the situation, decide what I wanted, and prepare myself to respond accordingly. The goal was to express my inner truth by helping the inside flow with the outside—making my wants and actions compatible.

INTUITION AND BOUNDARIES—INTERNAL LIE DETECTORS

Experiencing maternal narcissism included having blurred boundaries with my mother. I was an extension of my mom—not an individual with personal desires and goals. I grew into an adult who had no understanding of where I ended and others began. Not having boundaries, I constantly felt anxious because I didn't know what someone would do to me—or more accurately, what I would allow someone to do to me. The lack of boundaries meant I was powerless with others and ignorant to my intuition. Though I did not trust others most of the time, I did not trust myself to make decisions or set boundaries. I lived in a world feeling as if no one had my back, not even myself, and this made it a scary place. The bodily sensations I felt in my gut when something was not right is a nervous system response to threat—a sensation I was used to ignoring. I neither trusted it nor thought I had a right to defy it.

Boundary violations are wired in our body and alarm our conscience to act based on what we believe to be right or wrong. But over a long-time pattern of self-neglect, the inner voice of conscience became a faint whisper, and I was completely tuned-out—continuing to violate my boundaries by allowing others to violate them. I got accustomed to being uncomfortable and living with the physical sensations in my body: pounding heart, anxiety, a knot in my stomach, and chronic back pain. This was my body's way of trying to warn me something was wrong. These symptoms were the red flags I like to call my "lie detectors." They detect when I am not living in my truth—according to my wants and needs. The red flags or lie detectors also prompt me to examine whether my feelings and thoughts are true. When my lie detector goes off, I must stop to acknowledge it and ask myself, "I feel really_____. What is this about?" I first learned to *notice* (detect), then *apply the boundary* (live my truth). I had to make it a practice not to ignore or deny the signals in my body and to evaluate my situation, identify the boundary violation, then choose the best way to respond to gain and keep my self-respect. Living my truth further strengthens my internal lie detector.

Resentment is another emotional indicator/lie detector of a boundary violation. Once I feel irritable and resentful because of how others treat me, I realize it is partially my fault or my responsibility because I have not been exercising my boundaries, wants, and needs effectively, and others respond accordingly. If I feel resentful, I now ask myself, "Which boundaries have I *allowed* someone to ignore?" Part of setting boundaries is knowing what you want and asking for it. It is a skill I never developed because I grew up in an environment where boundaries were not respected. This newly formed skill of increased self-awareness enables me to explore my role in *setting* boundaries and *keeping* them.

REFRAMING—CHANGING PERCEPTION

How I saw, felt, and described my childhood experiences often differed from how my mother explained them. When I heard how she related our life events, it sounded as if we had not lived in the same house. Our memories and perceptions of our interactions and home life were at times complete opposites. She often described herself as always having protected me, but that was not my experience. So, which one was accurate? I asked my psychiatrist this question, and she said, "They both are." Her response baffled me, and I gave it a lot of thought. *If the difference lies in how we perceived the event, that means reality is your perception, so whose perception was correct? If Mom's perception were accurate, it would invalidate my entire emotional experience for many events and most of my childhood.* The thought of that crushed me.

Eventually, I realized there is truth in Dr. Vand's belief (that opposing perspectives both can be true) in some circumstances. Both experiences can be true. No one needs to be right or wrong, true or untrue. While we cannot dispute the reality of events and behaviors, our unique experience of the events and the motivation for our behaviors is *true for us.* The facts don't have to change, and we don't need to agree. Understanding this concept eliminated my conflicted feelings and need to prove my mother wrong. I could accept that even though our stories may not be identical, sometimes, my mother's experiences and mine are both valid. We were experiencing the same event differently—through different emotional and developmental lenses. Each experience held its own truth, so I could find peace, and that understanding decreased my need to fight for an external validation of my experience.

FORGIVENESS AND GRIEVING

Forgiving a perpetrator who has never expressed an apology was a difficult concept to wrap my mind around and an even harder one to apply. When your abuser and the source of your suffering was your parent, it can be extremely difficult to make peace with what happened. This is especially true if they have refused to take responsibility for their actions and deny you a sincere apology. Without this validation, it may feel impossible to heal. To illustrate this, my physiatrist related two vastly different scenarios posing the question of forgiveness:

Scenario 1: Imagine a friend ran over your foot with their car and broke it. They quickly stop to help you, express how sorry they feel, offer to pay any medical bills, and come to your house to cook and do housework. Would you be able to forgive them easily?

Scenario 2: Imagine a friend ran over your foot and broke it. They do not get out to help, and upon hearing your accusation, they deny it and say, "I didn't run over your foot; you must have done something else to it and don't remember. Why would you be standing that close to my car anyway?" Would it be easy to forgive this person?

It would be difficult to forgive the person in the second scenario and, even more so, to maintain a relationship with them. Having denied your experience and invalidated your pain, this type of breach produces a lack of trust and indicates their behavior will not change.

This battle of forgiveness was an internal fight I went to war with each day. For many years, I ached to tell my mother how I *really* felt—to confront her and remind her I hadn't forgotten how she treated me. I longed to hear her admit and take ownership of the pain and damage she had caused. As much as I wanted this closure, I could not bring myself to speak of it. I tried to move on with life, leave the past behind, and create a new adult relationship with Mom. Often, I was in a highly triggered state, filled with agitation and feeling trapped and voiceless. Becoming more and more curious about why I feared the confrontation with her, I pondered another question: What if I confronted her and didn't get the response I'd hoped for and experienced more rejection? The possibility of rejection could cost me everything I had, and I was afraid of losing her completely—I still needed her.

Hoping to move forward, I forgave my mother as if the situation were like the first scenario above, but it was more like the one described in the second scenario—without her apologizing and me pretending she did. I continued in the relationship, expecting her behaviors and characteristics would be different. Once again, I needed to prick the bubble and surrender into the acceptance of what our reality really was. In trying to accept, understanding the words of Louise Hay helped: "We need to understand that they, whom we most need to forgive, were also in pain."[18]

Knowing this truth led to another step in the healing process—grief. Allowing myself to grieve what was and what wasn't, I could get to a place of genuine acceptance and forgiveness. Recovery *is* grieving. We can grieve for the childhood we didn't have, the love that wasn't given, and the apology we'll never receive. Grief isn't always when someone dies—it can be for the parts of us that died while we were still alive.

VALIDATION AND SELF-COMPASSION

For as long as I can remember, I was continually seeking the approval of others, living for others' acceptance and "dying" if I sensed any rejection. When I first heard the word *validation*, I really did not understand what it meant or how the lack of it affected me. Validation confers *worth* and *legitimacy*. When something is valid, it may be trusted to be true, factual, and worthwhile. If you lack that inner sense of validation, you may question your very existence, feeling instead a deep numbness of mind, body and soul—an emptiness which may contribute to self-injurious behaviors, such as cutting oneself simply to feel *something*. After my diagnosis, I realized I had continued into adulthood by invalidating myself. I didn't trust my instincts and wouldn't accept my emotions. I was angry with myself for feeling a certain way, and I told myself I *shouldn't* have such feelings, or I became frustrated with myself, thinking, *Why do I feel this?* The question was not driven by curiosity but by shame. An inner monologue of should and shouldn't created a fierce resistance and barrier to my emotional development. I had to learn to *stop* resisting the emotions, *stop* working against myself and fighting against what is. The way my therapist expressed it was, I had to learn to stop "should-ing" myself. Having self-compassion needs to be the first response to our emotional experience. If we are compassionate with ourselves, the "should" or "shouldn't" language will cease. That critical language only creates more self-shame. I learned a truth that became a potent cure for this poisonous thinking: self-compassion is the antidote to self-shame.

11

DISCOVERING THE SECRET-SELF

When she transformed into a butterfly,
the caterpillar spoke not of her beauty, but of her weirdness.
They wanted her to change back into
what she always had been . . . but she had wings.

—Dean Jackson

For a while, therapy had become my full-time occupation, and secular work was a thing of the past. The friends I had were those with whom I was my chaotic self, and they often failed to see the positive work I was doing. Mockingly, some stated therapy was my new addiction. My father, who once had complained I worked too much, now said I was lazy for not working. It seemed no matter how hard I tried, I was never doing things right, and my efforts were never enough. My peers in group therapy, counselors, and the individuals I had met through a spiritual organization became more than professional support to me. They were like family and a source of encouragement not to give up.

During a therapeutic session with a drug and alcohol counselor, I was feeling rather defeated. Unable to make eye contact, I hung my head low for most of the session. Gently, she asked me to hold out my hand, and when I did, she placed a red solid glass heart in my palm. She said, "Keep this, and whenever you feel like giving up, hold on to this and say, I'm worth it." This fragile glass heart was like that of my own. It became a physical representation of her encouraging words and gave me a tool to use in distressing moments such as these—it helped prevent me from exercising what she called the *screw it muscle.*

I realized when you change things about yourself, even if it's for the better, people do not always accept it. When I no longer behaved in certain ways *with* or *for* others, the people in my life became puzzled and aggressive, and it felt like I was being forced back into a former role I didn't want to play. Perhaps my changes put others out of their comfort zone, revealing things about themselves they weren't ready to face. Harriet Lerner describes this phenomenon as a change-back or countermove in her book *The Dance of Anger.*[19] The phenomenon described my experience—it was like learning a new dance, trying to get in step with each other and into a new routine with the new me.

New Values—Spirituality

I noticed the dance of push-back behaviors from my family and peers, especially when I changed my life to align with my new spiritual values. When I had participated in Bible studies off and on over many years, occasionally, I had felt an inner happiness, connectedness, peace, and contentment I had never previously felt. I wanted to sustain this change, but these precious feelings were hard to maintain when the symptoms of my disorder knocked me down repeatedly. But part of me could get back up, and I was maintaining a spiritual routine; I realized spiritualty played an integral role in my wellness and life's purpose.

As I was changing my belief systems, I was also developing new values based on scriptural principles, and I made efforts to live in harmony with them. Formerly, I valued acceptance from others, which my decisions and actions reflected.

Belief systems and values work closely together. Values define what is most important to you and become a priority that guides your decisions—when lived up to, your values create an inward sense of integrity and self-respect. It has taken great humility to admit I needed a power greater than myself to maintain happiness—power from knowing and having a relationship with God became not only a value but a part of my basic needs. This is emphasized in Matthew 5:3 (NWT): "Happy are those conscious of their spiritual need."

The idea to follow your heart has won favor with many, but contrary to popular belief, this hasn't proven useful for me. My heart's desires have frequently caused me much pain and confusion. I've had more success when I use the Bible to include God's Word on matters—not just my heart—when making decisions. Jeremiah 17:9 (NWT) says, "The heart is more treacherous than anything else and is desperate."

It took years of work putting my new-learned truth into action through applying what I learned from the Bible and put on what Colossians 3:10 (NWT) calls "the new personality."

In James 1:22–24 (NWT), the Bible refers to itself as being like a mirror reflecting what is in our heart—our inner person. Just as we look into a mirror at our physical selves and can make adjustments to our appearance, we can use the Bible to see what is on the inside and make adjustments to our inner selves.

Scriptural insights have been a positive and essential tool in my recovery journey. They have proven to me that having and sticking to our values anchors us firmly so we don't drift away from our true selves.

Lessons from Vulnerability—Filling the Void of Chronic Emptiness

After a few years of therapy, I finally felt all my hard work had paid off when I heard Dr. Vand say, "You no longer qualify to have the disorder." Dr. Vand later requested I write my personal recovery story for people living with BPD for an upcoming book. Upon writing and submitting my short story, I learned it was accepted and eventually published in the book *Beyond Borderline: True Stories of Recovery from Borderline Personality Disorder.*[20]

Dr. Vand had warned me that sometimes some borderline traits and symptoms will still arise, and we can work through them—but regarding my personality, it was no longer "disordered." Soon after, I met my now husband, had a second child, and went back to school to work in the field of mental health. I terminated my sessions with Dr. Vand, and we shared a very special goodbye.

Upon my first year of marriage, triggers and BPD traits arose, and I still struggled to express myself. I often hid my tears from my partner, discreetly sobbing in our bed while he lay next to me. Sometimes, he said, "Be vulnerable with me," wanting to help carry some of my emotional burdens. Because I had my vulnerability exploited so much in my past, opening up was difficult for me. I practiced being vulnerable with him little by little, exposing parts of me I had kept hidden for so long. Each time I exposed a part of me, he met me with love and acceptance—never using it against me as I had experienced so often in past relationships. If I became triggered or dysregulated, he helped co-regulate me. Experiencing safe co-regulation by another helped dispel those negative, false beliefs and showed me it is safe to be seen and heard. This positive experience led me to finally form a secure attachment in a relationship. I felt more and more like myself, and it revealed a truth to me:

Self-acceptance + Vulnerability = Authenticity.

And when we are authentic, we can connect to ourselves and then others. Connection can heal many wounds.

Connecting with ourselves and others requires us to give voice to our inner experiences. Upon speaking to others with a BPD diagnosis in an online support group I facilitate, I asked them what trait they most struggle with. The answer most frequently given was "chronic emptiness." I asked my online community to explain, in their own words, what chronic emptiness meant and looked like to them.[21] Below are their responses:

"It's like a hole in my soul and no matter what you try to fill it with; food, alcohol, drugs, things I buy, relationships, it's always there. Like a void I need to fill but can't. It's a constant feeling that something is missing."

"It's like there's no marrow in my bones. It's like there's no substance to my limbs. Like walking around hollow and knowing that something needs to be inside of my structure but it's not there. And you don't know how to fill it or what to fill it with. You find something you think you can stuff in there to make yourself feel like you have substance but it slowly dissolves and you're left wandering, only to repeat the same process over and over."

"The battle between who I think I am and who I think I'm supposed to be. This feeling happens sometimes when I'm sitting with my friends. I'll feel as if I don't belong there, but I can't figure out where I do belong and I'm stuck in a chronic state of alienation and disconnection."

"Feeling alone in a room full of people, craving connection but it is far from me."

"A state of numbness."

"Not feeling sad but also not happy—feeling like you can't connect to people emotionally or physically."

"Like a donut, a hollow piece in the middle where a person should be."

"It makes me feel lost, as if I've lost everything even my identity; like a heavy fog of failure upon me."

"It's like the grass is always greener and it is impossible to get over the fence. All you can do is watch the beauty around you and you can't participate in it."

"The ability to cease to exist whilst still being alive."

These vulnerable expressions hold so much power. Vulnerability means to own your story, not run from it—it is your truth. I used to think it was my trauma history that separated me from everyone else, but it's what connects us—we can heal the isolation trauma brings by connecting to others through similar vulnerabilities. Once I put that knowledge into action, I experienced genuine connections with people, because it was only me speaking, free from seeking a false, self-serving acceptance. The deeper connections I felt from allowing vulnerability to work continued to shatter my false self and created a sense of inner-wholeness.

BECOMING ENOUGH

Many of the words used to describe the feelings of chronic emptiness were terms like *lost, hollow, numb, alone, missing, disconnected,* and *void.* They clearly resemble a disguised belief system of "I'm not enough." This not enoughness is the lie that fools many people, and believing it causes us to operate from a false self that can't seem to find genuine connection and contentment.

In his book, *The Angry Therapist: A No BS Guide to Finding and Living Your Own Truth,* John Kim states, "If you want to change your life, you have to change your beliefs, starting with your beliefs about yourself."[22] Kim also describes the false self as a "Pseudo Self" (i.e., not genuine), who seeks acceptance for a sense of security. He states that this pseudo self "allows you to hide and live in disguise." In contrast, he says the "solid self" requires you to stop living your lies.

The ability to challenge a core belief system is no easy task. Psychoanalyst and social philosopher Frantz Fanon explains it further:

Sometimes people hold a core belief that is very strong. When they are presented with evidence that works against that belief, the new evidence cannot be accepted. It would create a feeling that is extremely uncomfortable, called cognitive dissonance. And because it is so important to protect the core belief, they rationalize, ignore and even deny anything that doesn't fit in with the core belief.[23]

If you are an individual who can resist such cognitive dissonance through your new-found awareness, you must step out of your comfort zone, look at your truth, and tell yourself the new version if you want to instill new beliefs. Finding your truth comes from acceptance of self—all parts—and affirming within you an alternative belief system—a new story.

An affirmation is a statement that asserts something positive about yourself as true. The notion is if you repeat it to yourself long enough, you will believe it. In my online community, when someone joins the group, I ask: "What truths have you discovered about yourself?"[24] I am always inspired by the answers people write. I share some below:

"I am more than my illness."

"I can honor my feelings."

"That I do belong in my life, family and community."

"I'm real and I'm worth it, even when my mind doesn't tell me that."

"I am stronger than my impulses and triggers."

"I know I'm OK, not to take life too seriously and that freedom is possible."

"That I am worthy. That I am good enough."

"I am someone."

"I am allowed to be loved as I am while striving to evolve."

"I'm a good person."

"That we ourselves are the masters of our ships."

"That I've been a slave to my thoughts all along."

"That even though I have BPD, I am still worthy of love."

"I am an over-comer and stronger than I ever dreamed."

"That I am stronger than I think. I am a survivor and warrior because of my BPD."

"I am strong enough to heal."

"I am capable."

"That I am resilient."

"Being abused as a child was definitely not my fault."

"I can be loved without wearing a mask."

"That I have worth."

"I deserve to live."

These truths can lead us closer to our authentic selves— the self we are when we let go of who we think we should be. The self we are that shows self-love and self-compassion. The self we are that loves and accepts the good, the bad, the dark, and the light and knows we are enough, even though other people couldn't show us that truth before.

TIMING—THE PROCESS OF RECOVERY AND GROWTH

The untangling work involved in healing the past comes when we need it. My *ah-ha* moments often came at the right time. The light bulb turned on, and something finally clicked. This is my belief about the right timing for an aspect of recovery:

The right timing is when the person's measurable growth enables them to receive new information.

Throughout my recovery, I could have heard the same message a hundred times and never fully got the sense of it, but by being at the right stage of growth, I could hear that same message and finally attach meaning to it. Many books I refer to were a product of timing—learning things at the right stage of growth that enabled me to apply them. Therefore, one person's recovery cannot be sped up nor will it be identical to another's timeline. Timing is part of the unique process of growth and, as cliché as this may sound, trust the process.

FINAL WORDS—
RECOVERY AND BEYOND

Although I have been deemed *recovered* or disqualified for a diagnosis of borderline personality disorder, my journey is far from over. There are still areas in my life I am still recovering from and growing into.

I view recovery as a lifelong endeavor, which challenged me in writing this book because it felt as if it may never have an ending. As people, we are always learning, adapting, and growing. I am sure, even after completing this book, significant people will enter my life and events will take place and shape my growth in ways I can't imagine.

On the journey this far, I've learned to love my parents for who they were instead of hating them for who they weren't. I now see them as complex beings with many of their own traumas and perceptions, based on their own belief systems that their experiences had unconsciously formed. They hadn't had the opportunity to do the work I had done—the untangling work involved in finding one's truth buried beneath the trauma and the brain's protective systems.

Finding my truth freed me from the emotional slavery of victimhood and broke down the resistance to making lasting changes in my life and relationships. In these last few years, I formed new adult relationships with my parents. Doing so had its challenges and triggers. John Kim describes this phenomenon with his own parents, stating that he'd become instantly triggered when he saw his parents, even after many years of personal growth. He further stressed, the dynamic between family members was so strong it was as if he had become possessed to act according to the old family dynamic. Reverting back to the former family dynamic in this way, I've come to believe is born from the years of conditioning. Kim also suggests it can happen because our parents have not changed at all.[25] I managed to navigate through the conditioning and their lack of change (most of the time) to maintain a relationship with each of them.

A few years back, when I had become a single mother, my son was about a year old when my Dad moved in with me. Living together for the next six years, he watched me grow into the person I am today. He got to walk me down the aisle on my wedding day, and he got to be a grandfather again when I had my second child with my husband, who is also raising my son as his own. I feel at peace with the life we've created and the unique bond we share. I hold the relationship dear to my heart, especially now—reflecting on the time when Dad became suddenly sick with a very aggressive pancreatic cancer, and two weeks later, he took his last breath in my arms. Those last moments were spent staring into each other's eyes as I tried to find the right words to say goodbye and soothe his departure. A tear rolled down his cheek, and despite it all, the love we shared was proven in that moment.

My mother and I have become closer than I'd ever thought possible. I am still doing what I can to support her with her challenges—with the use of proper boundaries. Instead of trying to change or control her behaviors, I realize the power lies in me. By changing and controlling *my responses* to Mom, I can change the conditioned dynamics between us. Being able to change and control my responses is where I have found my power and the ability to love and accept her for who she is and acknowledge all she has endured in her life.

While reconnecting with your parents may not happen for you (or even be in your best interest), there are still ways to find power within your circumstances—only you can decide what that will look like. You are the designer. You are the narrator. Your truth awaits you. This is my story. This is my truth. It's time for you to find yours.

NOTES

1   *Diagnostic and Statistical Manual of Mental Disorders: DSM-5.* Washington, D.C.: American Psychiatric Association, 2017.

2   Bay Area CBT Center. "Schema Chemistry: The Entitlement/ Self-Sacrifice Trap." Accessed 12/30/2020. https://bayareacbt-center.com/schema-chemistry-entitlement-self-sacrifice-trap/.

3   McBride, Karyl. *Will I Ever Be Good Enough? Healing the Daughters of Narcissistic Mothers.* New York: Atria Paperback, 2013.

4   Ibid.

5   Ibid.

6   Ibid.

7   Levine, Amir, and R. Heller. *Attached: The New Science of Adult Attachment and How It Can Help You Find—and Keep—Love.* New York: Jeremy P. Tarcher/Penguin, 2011.

8   Ibid.

9   Ibid.

10   Ibid.

11   Ibid.

12   Porges, Stephen W. "The Polyvagal Theory: New Insights into Adaptive Reactions of the Autonomic Nervous System." *Cleveland Clinic Journal of Medicine* 76, no. 4 suppl 2 (2009). https://doi.org/10.3949/ccjm.76.s2.17.

13   Levine, Peter A., and Ann Frederick. *Waking the Tiger.* Berkeley, CA: North Atlantic Books, 1997.

14 Marzbani H., H. Marateb, and M. Mansourian. "Methodological Note: Neurofeedback: A Comprehensive Review on System Design, Methodology, and Clinical Applications." *Basic and Clinical Neuroscience Journal* 7, no. 2 (2016). https://doi.org/10.15412/j.bcn.03070208.

15 Koch, Liz. *The Psoas Book*. Felton, CA: Guinea Pig Publications, 1997.

16 Berceli, David. *Trauma Releasing Exercises (TRE)*. Charleston, SC: Booksurge Publishing, 2005.

17 Phillips, Maggie. "Working with Body Intelligence (BQ) and Self Attunement." Best Practices in Therapy. April 24, 2017. https://bestpracticesintherapy.com/2017/04/24/body-intelligence/.

18 Hay, Louise. *You Can Heal Your Life*. Carlsbad, CA: Hay House, 2010.

19 Lerner, Harriet. *The Dance of Anger*. New York: William Morrow Paperbacks, 2014.

20 Gunderson, John G., Perry Hoffman, ed. *Beyond Borderline*. Oakland, CA: New Harbinger Publications, 2016.

21 Anonymous responses from an online support group for people diagnosed with borderline personality disorder. December 2019.

22 Kim, John. *The Angry Therapist*. Berkeley, CA: Parallax Press, 2017.

23 Fanon, Franz. *Black Skin, White Masks*. London: Pluto Press, 2017.

24 Anonymous responses from an online support group for people diagnosed with borderline personality disorder. December 2019.

25 Kim, John. *The Angry Therapist*.

Made in the USA
Middletown, DE
04 September 2021

46902937R00076